New Games?

This is a collection of our favorite games. Some of them are brand new. Some have been played for hundreds of years. Many can be played competitively, with lots of opportunity for skill and strategy. Others have no object, really, besides getting people

together and enjoying each other. There are games here that you can play with one other person and games that a hundred can play.

As you read this book, you'll discover that what's new about these games is the *way* you play them. You can choose to compete because competition is fun, not because you're concerned with who wins. If you've all played hard and enjoyed it, then you've all won.

You can change the rules if you don't like them. So long as you all agree on what's fair, you can make the game into whatever you want it to be. Or you can invent a new one.

New Games is for everyone who wants to play. Your sex, age, or size doesn't determine your ability to have fun. And if everyone keeps in mind that the people are the most important part of the game, then no one has to be afraid of getting hurt.

But to really understand New Games you have to *play* them. Most of the games in this book are easy to learn and require very little equipment. All you need are a few of your friends and the desire to celebrate the day with play. In New Games there are no spectators.

The games we've collected here are just a beginning. Play them, change them, have fun with them.

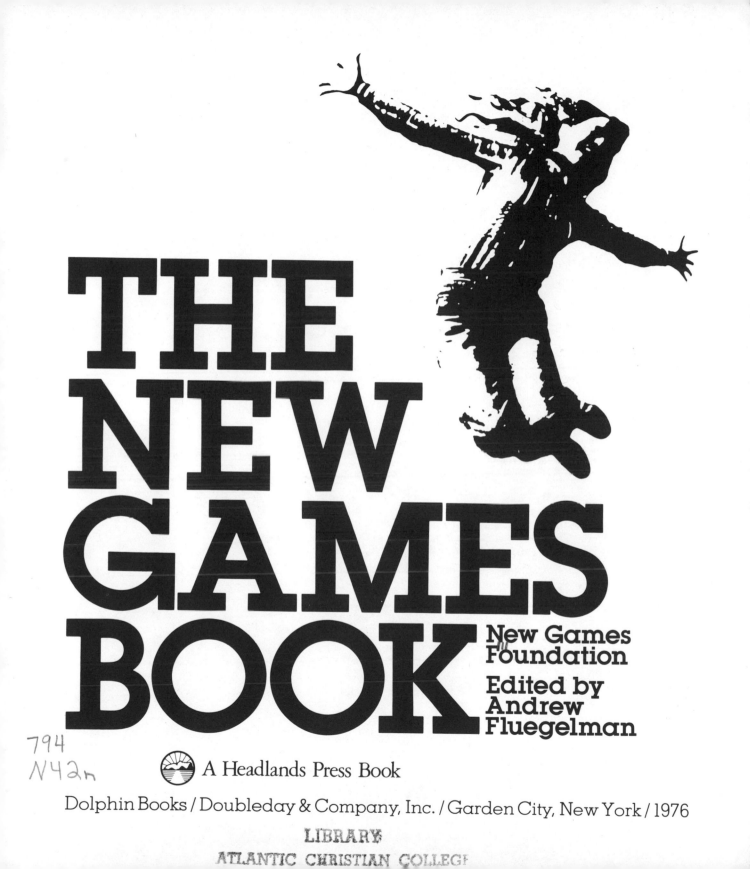

THE NEW GAMES BOOK

New Games Foundation

Edited by Andrew Fluegelman

A Headlands Press Book

Dolphin Books / Doubleday & Company, Inc. / Garden City, New York / 1976

Created and produced by The Headlands Press, Inc., Tiburon, California

Printed and bound by George Banta Company, Menasha, Wisconsin

Manufactured in the United States of America

Library of Congress Catalog Card Number 76-022654

ISBN 0-385-12516-X

Acknowledgment and thanks is made for permission to reprint material from the following:

The Ultimate Athlete
Copyright ©1974, 1975 by George Leonard
Reprinted by permission of The Viking Press, Inc.
The CoEvolution Quarterly, *Summer 1976*
Copyright ©1976 by POINT

15 14 13 12 11 10

Design Howard Jacobsen
Text Shoshana Tembeck
Andrew Fluegelman
Photography Ed Buryn
Andrew Fluegelman
Additional photography Ray Murray
Art Rogers
Larry Gertz
Ted Streshinsky
Alvan Meyerowitz
Jim Morgan
Joe Van Witsen
Ivan Olsen
Stewart Brand
Scott Bulkley
Carol Lee
Bob Samples
Games development John O'Connell
Games coordination Dale LeFevre
New Games consultant Burton Naiditch
Research Maxine Nunes
Copyreader Nancy Watkins
Photo lab Chong Lee
Illustrations Carol Kramer

Contents

It Began with World War IV

For Stewart Brand, San Francisco counterculture pioneer, playing New Games was another expression of his commitment to exploring new and more satisfying ways to live. This commitment had produced his Whole Earth Catalog, *first published in the late Sixties and later awarded the 1972 National Book Award. The* Catalog *provided "access to tools"—means by which people could realize their own visions of living, shape their environment accordingly, and share their adventure with others who were interested. When Stewart investigated how and why people play together, he saw in games the potential for another such tool. "Changing games seemed to me to be a useful thing to do, a way to be, a set of meta-strategies to learn."*

It is somewhat ironic that Stewart's inspiration for developing the first new games was the Vietnam War. "I felt that American combat was being pushed as far away as the planet would allow, becoming abstract and remote. It suggested to me that there was something wrong with our conflict forms here." So in 1966, when the War Resisters League at San Francisco State College asked him to stage a public event for

Stewart Brand

them, Stewart decided to create an activity which, instead of further entrenching people in their views and positions, would let them understand war by appreciating and experiencing the source of it within themselves. He called the event World War IV. It was to be a convergence of people at play.

Pacifists and war resisters in 1966 were opposed to warfare in any form, including competitive games. To test that opposition, Stewart designed a game that would give lots of opportunity to express aggression. "I invented it because all the peaceniks I was dealing with seemed very much out of touch with their bodies in an unhealthy way. Consequently, they were starting to project a heaviness on a personal level that was just as bad as the heaviness we were projecting in Vietnam. What I wanted was a game which would involve fairly intense physical interaction between players." Stewart gave his game the most offensive name imaginable—Slaughter.

Forty players entered the Slaughter arena—a large wrestling mat—on their knees and barefoot to minimize injuries. A rock band, on hand for the event, set off the action. Everything began happening at once. There were four moving balls, two moving baskets, and the stipulation that anyone could be "killed"—eliminated from the game—by being tossed bodily over the edge of the mat by the other players. There was no way for every player not to get involved. The game was intense, energetic, with much body contact and almost no injury. To the players' surprise, it was also fun.

But the major revelation that day resulted from a battle over the Earth. Stewart hauled out a six-foot diameter canvas and rubber pushball of the type he had played with in Army boot-camp training. This one had been painted with continents, oceans, and cloud swirls—the first Earthball. After a hundred or so people had donated their breath to inflate the giant ball, Stewart announced over a megaphone, "There are two kinds of people in the world: those who want to push the Earth over the row of flags at that end of the field, *and those who want to push it over the fence at the* other end. *Go to it."*

People charged the ball from both sides, pushing and cheering. Slowly it began to move, first toward one end, then back to the other. The game got hotter. There was plenty of competition, but something more interesting was happening. Whenever the ball approached a goal, players from the winning side would defect to lend a hand to the losers. Maybe it was, as Stewart commented, that "Berkeleyites can't stand to be on the overdog team," or perhaps that's just what happens when people find themselves playing together freely. Whatever the reason, that first Earthball game went on for an hour without a score. The players had been competing, but not to win. Their unspoken and accepted agreement had been to play, *as long and hard as possible.*

Out of his experience with these competitive *and aggressive games, Stewart conceived of "softwar," the idea that people could design their conflict* forms *to suit everyone's needs. Part of his inspiration had been T.H. White's fantasy,* The Once and Future King, *in which King Arthur reportedly got the armored rich people to stop clobbering the unarmored poor by luring all of the armored people into a "high tone clobbering club"—the Round Table. Stewart defined softwar as "conflict which is regionalized (to prevent injury to the uninterested),* refereed *(to permit fairness and certainty of a win-lose outcome), and cushioned (weaponry regulated for maximum contact and minimum permanent disability)." As Stewart later commented, "If you don't see much difference between softwar and sports, you're getting the point."*

Meanwhile, author George Leonard, Stewart's friend and fellow explorer, was beginning his own investigation into the nature of sports and play that would lead to his book The Ultimate Athlete. *But George was interested in aspects of the human potential other than the competitive. "Because our sports are so highly competitive, we may tend to believe that all human beings, especially males, are born competitors, driven by their genetic nature to the proposition that winning is 'the only thing.' The games of many cultures, however, have no competitive element whatever . . . Indeed, the notion that humans evolved only through grinding competition with nature and each other is a false one. Charles Darwin is clear on the point that, for the human race, the highest survival value lies in intelligence, a moral sense, and social cooperation, not competition."*

George Leonard was intrigued with the notion of "creative play"—the experience of a player placed in an open environment and encouraged to use his imagination to devise new play forms. For him, the relation of a person to the games he plays is of major significance. "Sports represent a key joint in any society," George wrote. "How we play the game may turn out to be more important than we imagine, for it signifies nothing less than our way of being in the world."

George Leonard and Stewart Brand began to exchange their ideas with others who were seeking alternatives to traditional sports. When they presented their new games and theories at the inauguration of the Esalen Sports Center in 1973, The New York Times reported that "the occasion may be to a change in sports what the storming of the Bastille was to the French Revolution." The time had come to play new games. Stewart, an impressario of free-form festivals and happenings, decided to stage a public tournament where people could create and share their games, and everyone could play.

To launch his proposed extravaganza, Stewart enlisted the aid of Pat Farrington, a woman well-versed in community organizing and committed to getting people working—and playing—together. The choice was a significant one for the future of New Games. To Stewart's vision of softwar, Pat added her own vision of "soft touch"—games that develop trust and cooperation.

"Games are not so much a way to compare our abilities as a way to celebrate them." Pat believed that by restructuring play, people could compete against their own limits rather than against each other. "I felt that by reexamining the basic idea of play, we could involve families, groups, and individuals in a joyous recreation experience that creates a sense of community and personal expression. People could center on the joy of playing, cooperating, and trusting, rather than striving to win."

Softwar, creative play, and trust—the union of these three approaches to playing was the seed point for the new games that were developing. The one element that they all shared was participation—by everyone.

By radio, poster, and flyer, the invitation went out for people to come and play at a New Games Tournament to be held on two consecutive weekends in October 1973 in Gerbode Preserve. This wild, open, 2200-acre valley just north of the Golden Gate Bridge had been made available by the Nature Conservancy, a Bay Area citizens group that purchases land available to developers and holds it for public use. They saw the New Games Tournament as an opportunity for the community

Pat Farrington

Gerbode Preserve, site of the First New Games Tournament

to relate to its natural environment in a new and creative way. With aid and encouragement from Huey Johnson, President of the Trust for Public Land, it was decided that the New Games Tournament would be the first public event held on the preserve.

The funds for this experimental sports spectacular were contributed by POINT, the truly non-profit foundation that had been set up to distribute the proceeds from The Last Whole Earth Catalog. *In typical Stewart Brand style, the foundation had been created with built-in obsolescence, distributing not only its interest, but its capital as well, to inventive and worthy projects that had no assurance of success and that* didn't *apply for funding.*

"All tournament-goers are invited to bring their own new games," the announcements read. "Any person or group that wants to challenge anyone else to any reasonably weird event at the Tournament is hereby encouraged." The chance to participate, not only by playing, but by actually making up new games, attracted 6000 people, each paying $2.50 adult admission to the gargantuan playland at Gerbode. Educators, authors, and children came, as well as land acquisition and management personnel, officials from local parks and recreation departments, social service specialists, students, and people simply out for a good time. The Hog Farm, a traveling commune, catered the food, and the U.S. Army supplied kitchens and water tanks.

The bare hills of Gerbode, covered only with the parched grasses of summer, had suddenly burst into color. Banners and streamers filled the air; elegant canvas structures spread their wings over food and refreshment concessions. In their shade, people played chess, parcheesi, and go, while waiting to try their hands and eyes at the electronic computer blips of Space Race and Pong. Among the folds of an expansive orange and white parachute bobbed hundreds of balloons. Mimes, clowns, minstrels, and jugglers paraded across the fields and slopes. And, soaring 2000 feet above it all, looking like a migration of butterflies, were red, gold, and green hang-gliders. It was a fifty-ring circus, but no one was watching—everyone was playing.

Beyond the tents, the "real stuff" of the Tournament was taking place—the new games everyone had brought to play. Earthball and Slaughter were there, taking their places next to People Pass, the Lap Game, and the Bone Game. George Leonard brought his own version of Frisbee, encouraging players to venture beyond what they saw as their own limits and to call their own points besides. Some traditionally competitive games had been restructured to emphasize play rather than winning. The chant from Infinity Volleyball crescendoed to "48 . . . 49 . . .50!" before the ball—along with a few players—fell to the ground. The final score was shared by both teams.

Some gamesters from the annual Renaissance Pleasure Faire perched people on foot-square platforms to play one of their favorite games, Hunker Hawser, and a ten-year-old boy got a whole mass of grown-ups wriggling around on their stomachs in Snake-in-the-Grass. In some games, it was the change of scale that made them new and exciting. Over a hundred people lent their pull in a giant Tug of War that stretched a 400-foot ship's hawser across a creek. Following a wild Le Mans start, everyone became gripped in a straining stalemate, until one side finally gave way and the dozens of whooping children from the losing side got a free ride across the water on a people-powered rope tow.

People were also enjoying the chance to let out their aggressions. Resounding whacks of polyethylene Boffers popped the air, while nearby, players perched on wooden rails took to joyfully whopping each other with straw-filled sacks. Wavy Gravy, one of the original Merry Pranksters, weaved in and out of it all, reminding everyone that the only fast rule

was "Play Hard, Play Fair, Nobody Hurt."

No one had really forseen what beauty and power could be created by people at play in an atmosphere that encouraged spontaneity and participation. "I was struck by the happy abandon on the faces," George Leonard noted. "Contrast a lovely valley full of games with all the bodies slumped before TV sets on that same afternoon." Everyone had rediscovered their bodies and imaginations. As the participants limped out the gate at nightfall, arm-in-arm, perhaps nursing a bruise or two, they talked excitedly about returning the next day. People had experienced the joy of playing together. They had become part of a play community which they had helped create.

In terms of delight alone, the tournament had been an unqualified success—but not just for the six thousand people who had played on the land. When the four-day tournament was over, the native residents of Gerbode Preserve—the crickets, deer, hawks, and field mice—found their home intact. The site had been left as it had been entered. According to Pat Farrington, "The concept of a joyous and harmonious interaction between people and land resources is one of the foundations of New Games. One of our major goals is to make people aware of public lands and to promote interest in maintaining them and using them in an ecologically sound manner. New Games is attempting to bring people into harmony with their environment once again."

But New Games were still simply new games, and the tournament was over. With characteristic detachment, Stewart Brand returned to editing the Whole Earth Epilog, *sequel to* The Last Whole Earth Catalog, *and to launching his "journal of conceptual news,"* The CoEvolution Quarterly. *Pat stayed on to wind up a few details of the event, POINT funds were allocated to complete the film of the Tournament which Tom Schneider had been commissioned to produce, and that was essentially to be the end of the project. "The Tournament was one test tube in one laboratory at one time," Stewart told a reporter from* Sports Illustrated. *"We organized it to see what happens when you say, 'Hey, new games, folks.'"*

What had happened wasn't going to be dropped that casually, however. Ray Murray, from the Federal Bureau of Outdoor Recreation in San Francisco, had managed to get to the final day of the tournament. What he had seen there looked like a way to breathe new life into national urban park and recreation programs. "In too many parks, the recreation leader had become the person with the key-ring on his belt. He was there to open the locker rooms, the equipment cage, to turn the lights on and off, but he had forgotten how to work with people and get them simply playing together. A lot of green spaces in our parks weren't being used. These new games, with minimal impact on the environment and no need for permanent structures or specialized equipment, could be worked into programs that would involve all members of the family in active recreation—and it could be done almost anywhere."

Ray invited Pat Farrington to talk to his department about the Tournament and New Games. After the meeting, a few excited people remained to encourage Pat to develop the concept, but for her, the Tournament had been only a prototype for others to learn from. With a final "Thanks anyway," Pat left for home. Ten minutes later, she was back: "Hey, maybe we do have something here." New Games had begun.

Pat and Ray realized they would have to establish some credentials for New Games if they were to reach the professionals in physical education, parks and recreation, and social services. With a few enthusiastic workers functioning as the "New Games Staff," Pat began responding to requests from schools and community organizations wanting to know more about what they had experienced at the Tournament. In the spring of 1974, the first break came. A physical education student from the University of California at Hayward approached Ray Murray, wishing to work with the Bureau of Outdoor Recreation on a project. Ray suggested a conference on New Games, and then proceeded to invite officials from all the park and recreation programs in the Bay Area.

New Games had made it into the classroom, but the Hayward conference wasn't just another lecture course. More than 300 students and professionals found themselves creating games out in the audience or playing new ones up on stage. The whistles and rulebooks of traditional recreation were cast aside as everyone participated, communicated, flowed with the changes, and felt the joy of body, mind, and spirit joined in play. Many found support for what they had always felt but had not known how to put into action. Two of the most enthusiastic were Marcelle Weed, of the Oakland Parks and Recreation Department, and Sue Sunderland, a faculty member in Hayward's recreation department. "It let us know that we weren't all crazy," they agreed. "We had always felt that it just wasn't right for only five people out of a class of four hundred to be able to play 'on the team.'" As a result of the conference, ten park and recreation departments scheduled New Games workshops, and by that summer New Games were being played in several local parks.

Pat also saw the potential, and the need, for New Games to reach communities at the grassroots level. The first major opportunity came when the All People's Coalition, a strong and active federation of community groups in San Francisco's Visitacion Valley area, initiated a work project to renovate a local playground. Visitacion Valley is a residential neighborhood on the fringe of San Francisco, populated by blacks, Latinos, Samoans, and whites living on low to middle incomes. Public recreation programs were literally nonexistent there, and since no one felt a part of the Visitacion Valley playground, it was frequently vandalized. Feeling that cooperative play could foster an attitude of cooperative work, the Coalition asked New Games to be part of its renovation program and set off the project with a one-day tournament at the playground.

On the morning of the event, a red pick-up truck, mounted with a bullhorn and bearing two Earthballs, drove through the streets of Visitacion Valley, gathering children like the Pied Piper. By the time the tournament was in full swing, 400 children were playing—the most intensive use of the area that long-time residents had ever witnessed. Even the young men of the neighborhood, who usually used the playground as a place to hang out and drink beer, stopped scoffing at the activities and joined in the games. The divisions within the neighborhood had not been erased, but on that day the fighting took place with Boffers instead of knives, and the "softwar" ended when everyone agreed it was over. At the end of the day, a spirited round of Eco-Ball left the playground cleaner than before the tournament had begun.

What was most significant about the Visitacion Valley event was that the racially fragmented neighborhood had all met on one day in one place. For children used to experiencing play as a school for survival, playing just for fun was a new game in itself. The young people of Vis' Valley continued to play New Games as they worked to redesign their playground, and now a public space, formerly closed eighty percent of the time, is alive with children clambering over tire nets and parading across suspension bridges in a community play area custom-designed by its users.

Buoyed by the success of these two events, Pat and the New Games staff committed their efforts to completing arrangements for the Second New Games Tournament, scheduled to be held that May 1974, once again at Gerbode

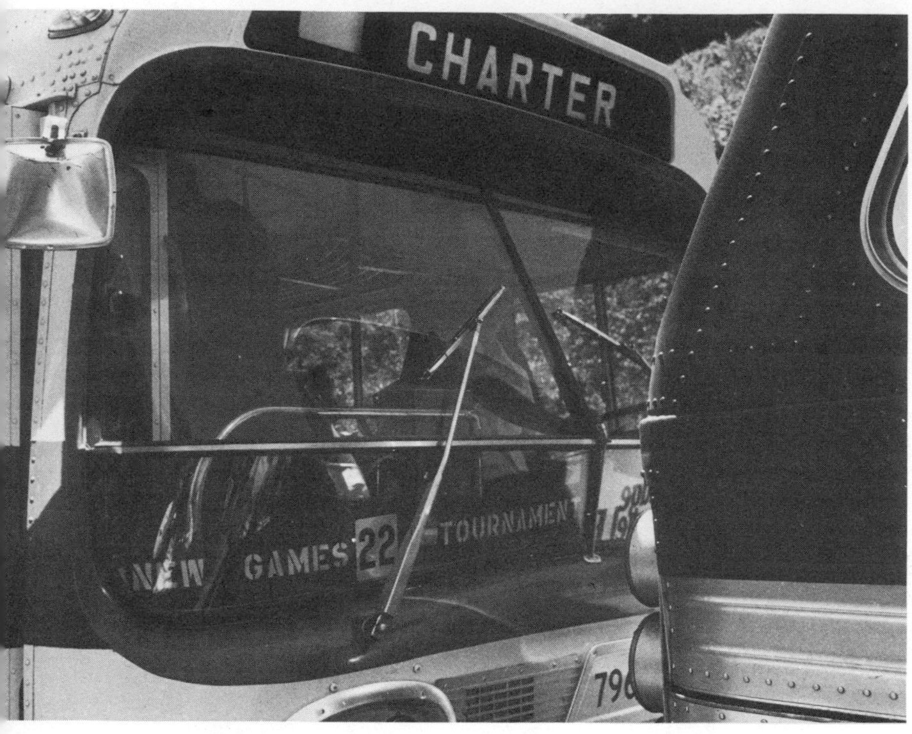

Preserve. Although the participants at the First Tournament had included people of all ages, both sexes, and varied backgrounds, the majority had been middle-class, white, long-haired males in their twenties and thirties. They had probably been playing new games for years. Had that accounted for the First Tournament's success? The staff had seen the power of play to cut across cultural barriers in the smaller settings, however, and they were convinced that a large-scale, cross-cultural event would succeed as well.

New Games visited community groups in the Bay Area, showing them the film made at the First Tournament and inviting them to help create and participate in the planned event. By the day of the Tournament, over thirty community groups had donated materials and personal services, and several local businesses and foundations had made monetary contributions to the event, supplementing POINT's funding.

A major innovation with the Second Tournament was the decision to set up a public transportation system to the event. Part of the motivation was environmental—private vehicles would not be permitted to congest the natural setting. The prime consideration, however, was that people who had no transportation of their own would be able to get out of the city to play. Each day of the Tournament, free charter busses left from urban community centers for Gerbode. Visitacion Valley itself filled four vehicles daily. Those who crossed the Golden Gate Bridge in cars were directed to reach the Preserve by shuttle bus from a nearby town, and public transit lines ran busses from downtown San Francisco to the Tournament.

The Second Tournament featured all the new physical games of the first event, but it also included activities that emphasized group and family participation. Tournament-goers were encouraged to bring along lunches for old-fashioned family picnics. The foods available at the concession stands were ethnic in origin so that people of different cultures could learn more about each other. There was face-painting, sticks and glue for group sculptures, and macramé hangings that everyone worked on.

At the trampolines, lent by the Berkeley YMCA, people

waiting their turn were encouraged to stand by as spotters. During the four days of nonstop leaping and bouncing, no one was hurt. Children had to enlist the help of new friends to sail the ten-foot kites—trying to fly them alone meant the possibility of going along for the ride. Some games, like sack racing, were familiar. Others, like Dho-Dho-Dho, were a completely new exerience for everyone.

This time New Games received national coverage through the media. Walter Cronkite featured the Tournament on his CBS Evening News, and ABC-TV made a five-minute film for their award-winning children's series, "To Make A Wish." Peter Weinberg, producer of the film, was so taken with New Games that when the staff later visited New York City for an event, he made available telephones, office space, and an "equipment depot" in a midtown Manhattan high-rise.

New Games had by now received its tax-exempt status as a foundation, and it looked like it was off to a spectacular start. A barrage of requests for training programs was coming in from urban recreation departments, physical education programs, conservationists, and community centers. However, the Second Tournament, originally intended to set the Foundation on its feet financially, left it instead with an $18,000 deficit. While Penny Gerbode-Hopper made lifesaving contributions to cover operating costs, a handful of dedicated people willing to work sixty-hour weeks for deferred salaries stretched themselves to cover the events.

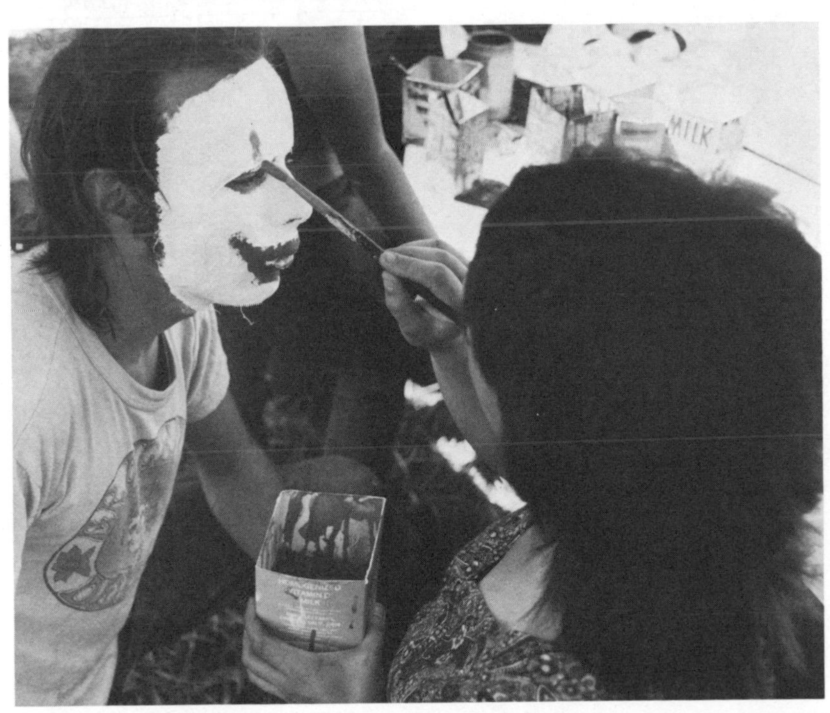

New Games caught on wherever they were tried. A New Games workshop at the Western Regional Conference of the Association of Humanistic Psychology got three hundred professional counselors playing all afternoon in an event they later voted their favorite at the conference by a margin of three-to-one. At the annual meeting of the National Community Educators Association, the New Games staff capped four days of playing and creating games by dropping a thousand superballs from the ceiling of the Continental Ballroom of the San Francisco Hilton. No wonder the participants called it the "the liveliest NCEA conference ever."

Meanwhile, preparations were underway for the Third New Games Tournament, to be held in May 1975 in San Francisco's Golden Gate Park. If a full-scale event had worked in the country for an urban population, why not play right in the city itself? This urban festival was billed as a celebration of Golden Gate Park by its owners—the people of San Francisco. Radio spots and flyers in Spanish, English, and Chinese announced, "We are coming together to celebrate our cultural, racial, social, and chronological differences." *This time New Games' interest in bringing people into harmony with their environment meant not only the environment of land and air, but also the atmosphere created by the population of a city.*

Everyone was now convinced that free admission to the event suited the nature of New Games. Families of all sizes, unrestricted by cost, could play together. Passers-by, intrigued by the games, could involve themselves spontaneously. And restricted funds, coupled with no admission revenue, discouraged fancy excesses and encouraged creative scrounging and contributions from

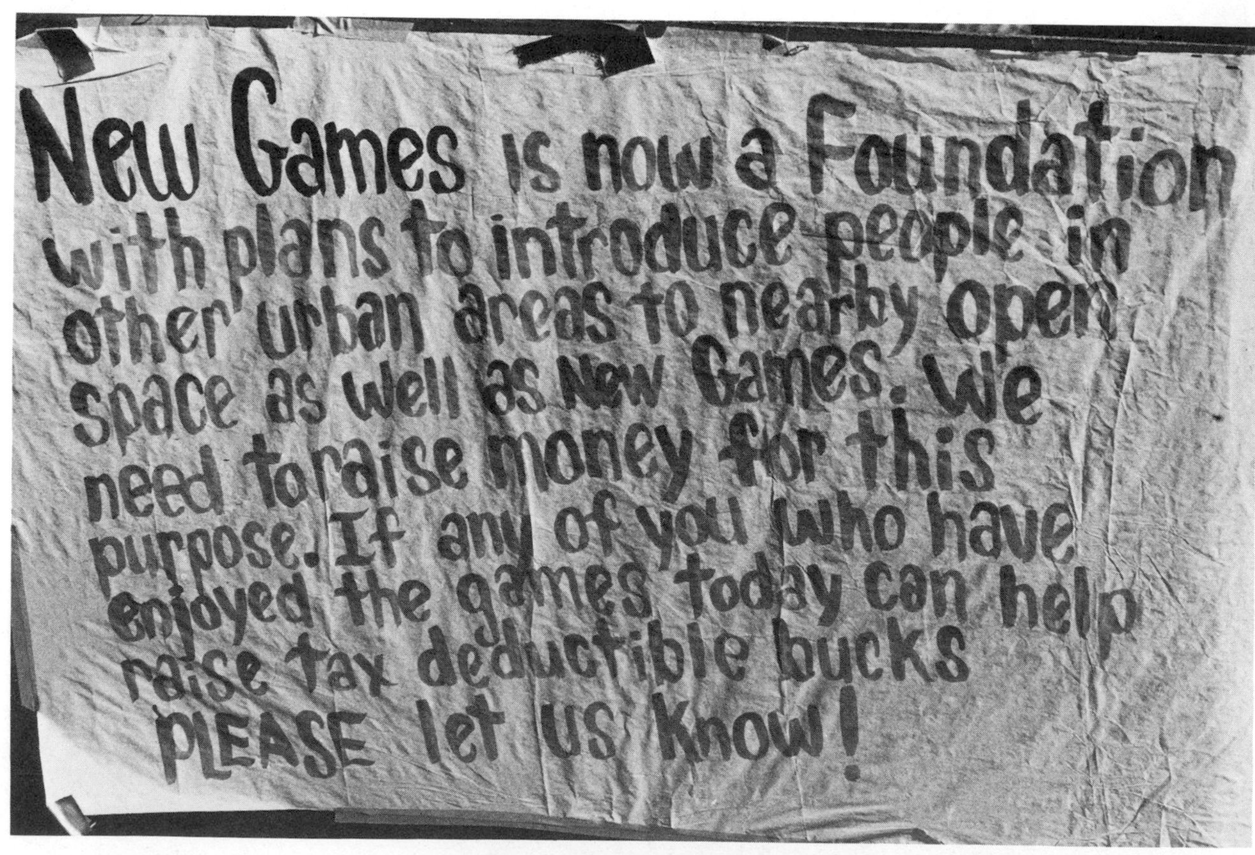
New Games is now a Foundation
with plans to introduce people in
other urban areas to nearby open
space as well as New Games. We
need to raise money for this
purpose. If any of you who have
enjoyed the games today can help
raise tax deductible bucks
PLEASE let us know!

community groups. Major funding for this event came from the San Francisco Foundation, a community trust that found New Games to be exactly the kind of activity they wished to promote. In all, over 120 community groups participated, from radio stations and businesses to growth centers and church groups.

In contrast to the casual country miles of Gerbode, the thirty city acres of Speedway Meadows in the Park occasioned a lively and concentrated affair. The ten thousand people who came to play that day found themselves stacked and squeezed between strangers in a precarious People Pyramid, tumbled into a tangle of Knots, and spun off with their neighbors into a giant Spiral. The rope in Tug of War never went slack as new people joined in and others moved on. Still, there was space to lie in the sun with friends, listening to stories, or to design finger-painted masterpieces in the shade of canvas shelters.

Amazingly, there were only forty official referees there to lead the games. Once a game got started, a referee would hand an enthusiastic player a megaphone and say, "Why don't you run the next game?" The chance to be in charge of the low-key officiating was always eagerly accepted, and in turn passed on to another player for the following game. Referee T-shirts were for sale at the New Games information booth, and by the middle of the day, the Tournament looked like a convention of playing referees. By now everyone had realized that the games were all theirs—to create, to officiate, and to play. The event ended with what must have been the greatest public pie fight ever held in San Francisco.

New Games tournaments and workshops are now springing up all over the country. People in Arizona, Michigan, Boston, Georgia, Minnesota, Texas, and Washington, D.C., have picked up the idea and fashioned their own events. New Games is also gaining an international reputation. The Ministry of Youth, Sport, and Recreation in Melbourne, Australia, invited Pat Farrington to develop a New Games program for the State of Victoria. The government provided her with a staff of twenty-five referees and a fleet of four vans to roam the countryside like modern versions of Johnny Appleseed, planting New Games as they go. New Games also spanned the Atlantic when the Open University in Brighton, England, invited New Games to help put on a full-scale tournament there in July 1976.

In may cases, park and recreation officials have initiated the contact with New Games. But more significant than this "official" recognition is the interest in New Games that is arising, as did the games themselves, from the grassroots. Families and neighborhoods are seeking the playful contact of Sunday afternoon celebrations. Teachers and students are creating an environment where everyone can learn simply by playing hard and fair. Therapeutic recreation leaders are bringing people out of institutions and into parks to play games in which everyone can participate. New Games is appealing to people who are not waiting for someone else to entertain them—people who want to experience their own experience.

Headquartered in a neighborhood storefront office in San Francisco, the core New Games staff and a dedicated group of volunteers are busy organizing workshops and trainings and acting as consultants for tournaments being planned in other communities. They also publish a newsletter to keep everyone informed of the best ways to acquire or make New Games equipment, news from New Games enthusiasts around the nation and the world, and the best new New Games. "We play in the office, too," affirms Burton Naiditch, the New Games Foundation's Executive Director. "We run the Foundation like a New Game. After a while it just becomes a way of life."

The games themselves have evolved as the many people who have enjoyed them have in turn shared their ideas with the Foundation. Well over half the games included in this book were not played at either of the first two tournaments. Burton foresees that in a couple of years over half the games played as "New Games" will be other than those presented here. "There is an infinite number of New Games—by the time people have played the ones we have suggested, the only true new games will be those still to be invented."

New Games is not a list of suggested forms and structures. Nor is it a foundation dedicated to perpetuating itself. New Games is an attitude that encourages people to play together. To learn only the form and not grasp the essence would be to miss the lifeline that gives rise to that attitude. The purpose of the New Games Foundation is to serve as a focal point for fostering and communicating this concept.

Solely for the purpose of having fun, we can be free and foolish in the arena of New Games and let the spirit carry us. Everything else the games may serve will follow naturally. ■

New Games in Melbourne, Australia

Games for Two

VERY ACTIVE
Tweezli-Whop
Boffing
Schmerltz

ACTIVE
New Frisbee
Hunker Hawser
Fraha

MODERATE
Stand-Off
Aura
Frisbee Golf

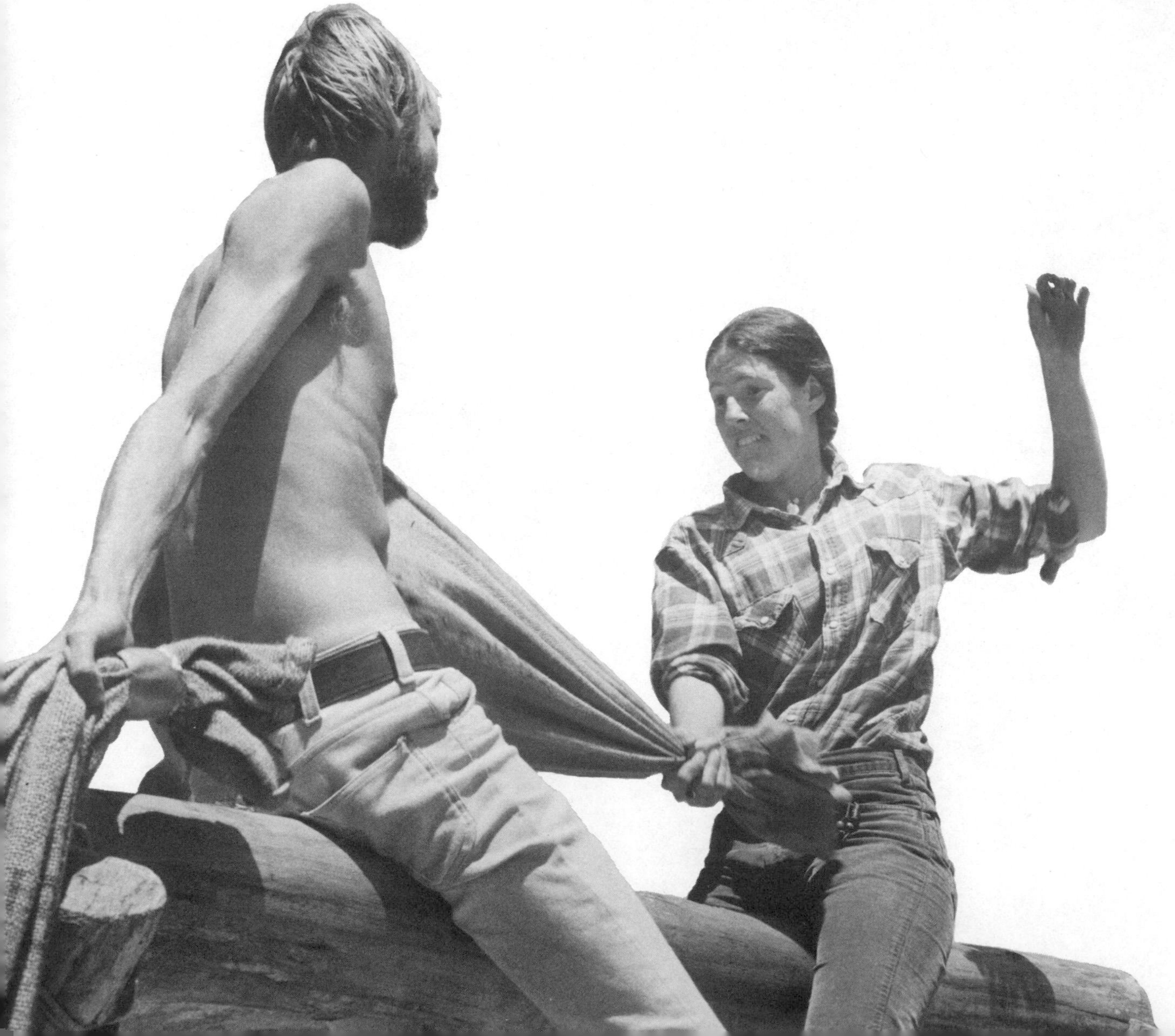

Tweezli-Whop

If the name "Tweezli-Whop" doesn't give you a very clear picture of what this game is about, try "Toodle Dooping." That's what it's called in Wyoming. Under either name, you might recognize it best as an offspring of classical "Pillow Fighting." Only it's a little more down-home.

You'll need two burlap sacks filled with straw and a wooden rail perched high enough to keep your feet from touching the ground. The area beneath the rail should be generously cushioned—a minor haystack will do. You and your partner straddle the rail, face-to-face, and have a go at "whopping" each other with the sacks until one (and frequently both) fall off.

Besides being great fun, this is a terrific way to work out tensions. A husband-wife team might want to give it a go sitting back-to-back, while business associates might try it with one hand behind their backs. How about side-saddle? Whichever way you try it, sooner or later you'll be hitting the hay. ■

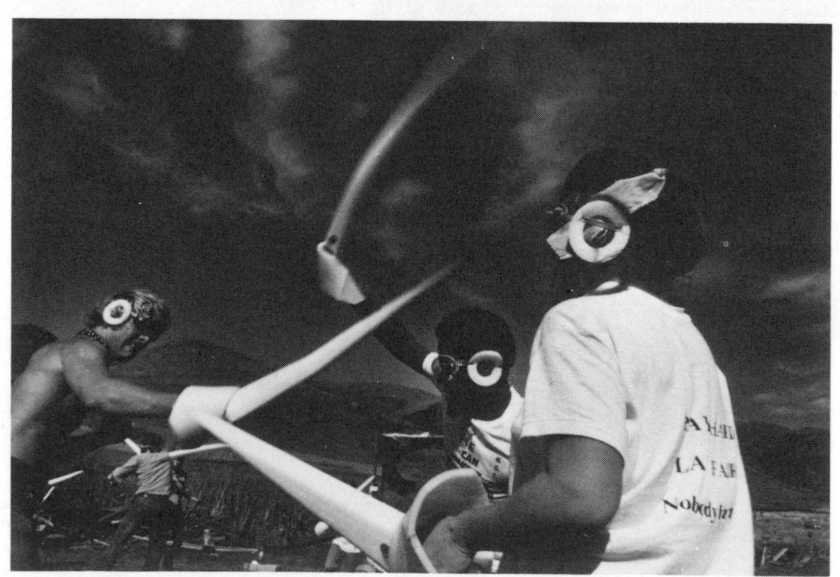

Boffing

"En Garde!" The foils are drawn. The first blow lands with a resounding *Boff*. "Take that, you varlet!" Foam flashes in the sunlight. Thwack. Pop. "Yield or die, knave!" Squunch. The battlefield lies strewn with giggling bodies.

Boffing was invented by a fellow with the appropriately dashing name of Jack Nottingham. Stewart Brand thinks he should be nominated for a Nobel Peace Prize.

A Boffer is a three-foot duelling sword made of polyethylene foam, supplied with protective eye and ear guards. (See page 190 for information on how you can make or buy your own.) You can flail away at your opponent, unleash years of pent up aggression, and both preserve your corporeal well-being. You might get your ego dented a bit, though, if you drop your defense and let yourself be boffed in the belly by your opponent's rapier.

Actually, the classic rules of Boffing discourage wild swiping and pounding, provide that hits must be made between the shoulder and the waist, and award points only for a well-placed thwack with the tip of your sabre that produces a distinctive popping sound. All are warned, however, that chivalry appears to be dead. Don't expect a soft touch or any mercy at the hands of your lady friend, and you're certain to be boffed into submission if you chance to run into a Children's Crusade. ■

Schmerltz

Ted Dreyfus and Pete Whiteley invented this wonderful homemade toss-and-catch missile. It's without doubt the best new "ball" we've seen since the Frisbee.

To make your Schmerltz, get a long, cotton "tube sock" without a heel (hiking supply stores carry them) and a solid, sponge rubber softball (about a dollar at variety stores.) Drop the ball into the toe of the sock, tie a knot just above the ball, and *voilà!* You've got yourself a genuine Schmerltz.

Now take it to your local park and start tossing. The official Schmerltz toss is made by holding the end of the sock, twirling the Schmerltz around underhand a few times, and letting it sail when you've reached critical velocity. With a bit of practice, you'll be able to send it flying to your partner, streaming like a comet.

The only acceptable way to catch a Schmerltz is to grab it out of the air, *one-handed*, by the tail *only*. You'll probably have to work on perfecting your catch, but once you get it down, you'll marvel at being able to snag what seems to be nothing more than the shadow of the leading ball.

There are probably some great games you could invent for your Schmerltz, but, like Frisbee, we've yet to get tired of simply playing catch with it. ■

New Frisbee

Old Frisbee itself is still a relatively new game. Yet there are probably very few of you who haven't given the disk a toss at some point. If you have counted yourself too inelegant for the graceful game of Frisbee or too skilled to find a gameful match, take heart. George Leonard's New Frisbee gives points simply for honest effort. (That's George pictured on the facing page, making an honest effort at executing a perfect semi-crouch toss.)

The only requirements for play are willingness to stretch yourself to the limit and "impeccable personal morality," as George terms it. The basic game is the same as any other Frisbee game—throwing and catching. The difference lies in the scoring.

To start, both players declare which hands they will use for throwing and catching. They may throw with one hand and catch with the other, but this must remain constant throughout the game.

The player who catches determines the points for both himself and the thrower. Each time the Frisbee is launched, the catcher makes an all-out effort to reach and catch it. If even his best efforts—including diving and leaping—can't get him in touch with the flying Frisbee, the catcher gives himself one point. If the Frisbee's flight is direct and accessible, and yet the catcher misses it, he gives one point to the thrower. The thrower graciously accepts all decisions, and gets ready to catch the Frisbee now hurtling in her direction.

The thrower gets two points if the catcher reaches the Frisbee but then fumbles and drops it. There's also an incentive for the thrower to master his technique. If the Frisbee tilts more than forty-five degrees from the horizontal during its flight, the catcher can call out "Forty-five!" and award herself one point.

The bonus twist of newness in New Frisbee comes when the throw is good and the catcher makes a clean catch with the declared hand. In this situation, no points are received by either player. The perfection in that action is the reward in itself.

All knowledgeable observers of New Frisbee matches are encouraged to applaud good plays and good calls. While they cannot interfere with the decisions of the catchers, their own responses might help a catcher evaluate his limitations—or lack of them. Besides the fun involved, New Frisbee is a good way to explore and define your own boundaries, and a great warm-up for George Leonard's Game of Games. ■

Hunker Hawser

This game is sure to prove that "the harder they come, the harder they fall." If you like one-on-one competition, here it is—along with a real surprise as to what gets you off your pedestal.

Pedestals are about six inches high and small enough so that players can't move their feet without losing balance. (A good mount might be a block of wood or styrofoam, a tree stump, or try an overturned pot of the cooking, flower, chimney, or even chamber variety.)

Players hunker down on their platforms, which are set about six feet apart, each holding one end of a rope about one inch in diameter and at least fifteen feet long. The excess rope lies coiled between them—but not for long.

At the starting signal, the players begin reeling in. The object is to unbalance your opponent by tightening or slackening the rope. Sound simple? "Oh I'll just give a good pull and. . ." Suddenly your opponent relaxes her hold, and over you go in a spectacular backward somersault—defeated by your own energy. In fact, the more aggressive you become, the more vulnerable you are. The whole idea of how to win becomes as topsy-turvy in this game as the chamber pot on which you're standing.

We've been hankering to know what Hunker-Hawser would be like with three people and a Y-shaped rope. Or lots of hunkerers and a circular rope. If you try, let us know. ■

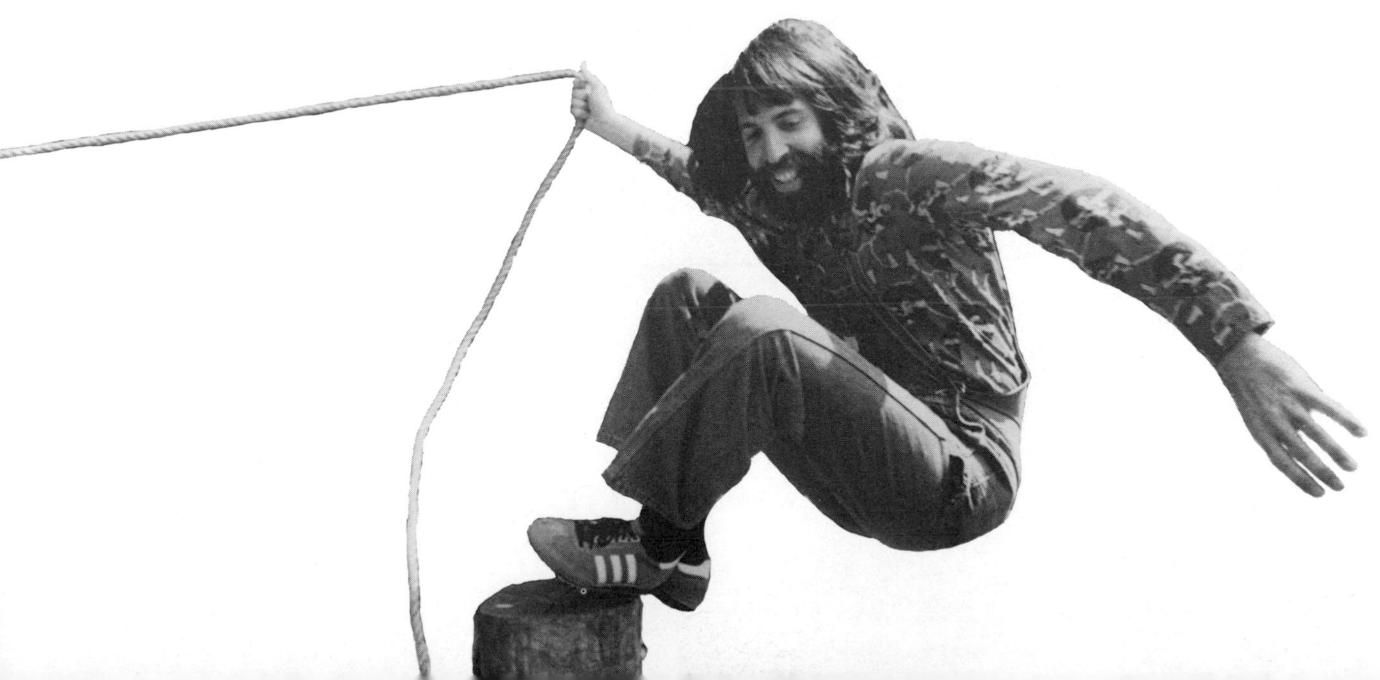

Fraha

This ancient game originated in the eastern Mediterranean and is now popular in South America, where it's called *Las Paletas*. The name Fraha was given to the game by one of the companies that make equipment for it. (See page 190 for information on how you can make or buy your own.) You'll need two solid wooden paddles about the size and weight of those used for paddleball, a hard ball (a squash ball is perfect), and a friend.

Begin standing about 5 to 10 feet apart. Hit the ball lightly to your partner. Have her return it to you. Try for high, arching shots, and see how long you can keep the ball in play. When you get the feel of the paddle and the ball, experiment by varying the distance between you, hitting the ball on a more direct line, or limiting the number of steps you allow yourself to make the return.

Fraha is a game of cooperation, but there's much competition involved. You and your partner are both competing against the Universe's seemingly insatiable appetite for disorder. To overcome that, you'll have to enlist the aid of the Universe's other great principle—harmony.

As you play, try to build a spirit channel between you and your partner, and help the ball to travel it. When you can *feel* this channel, it will seem that the *only* place the ball can go is straight to your partner's paddle. You might even feel as though the ball, paddles, and players are all caught by a powerful, independent force. To preserve this force, you'll both have to stay in tune with the game and each other. Concentrate too hard, though, and you'll likely break the channel.

Because Fraha is a game that has been stripped to its essentials, it's particularly easy to experience this feeling of harmony. Discover it in other games. ■

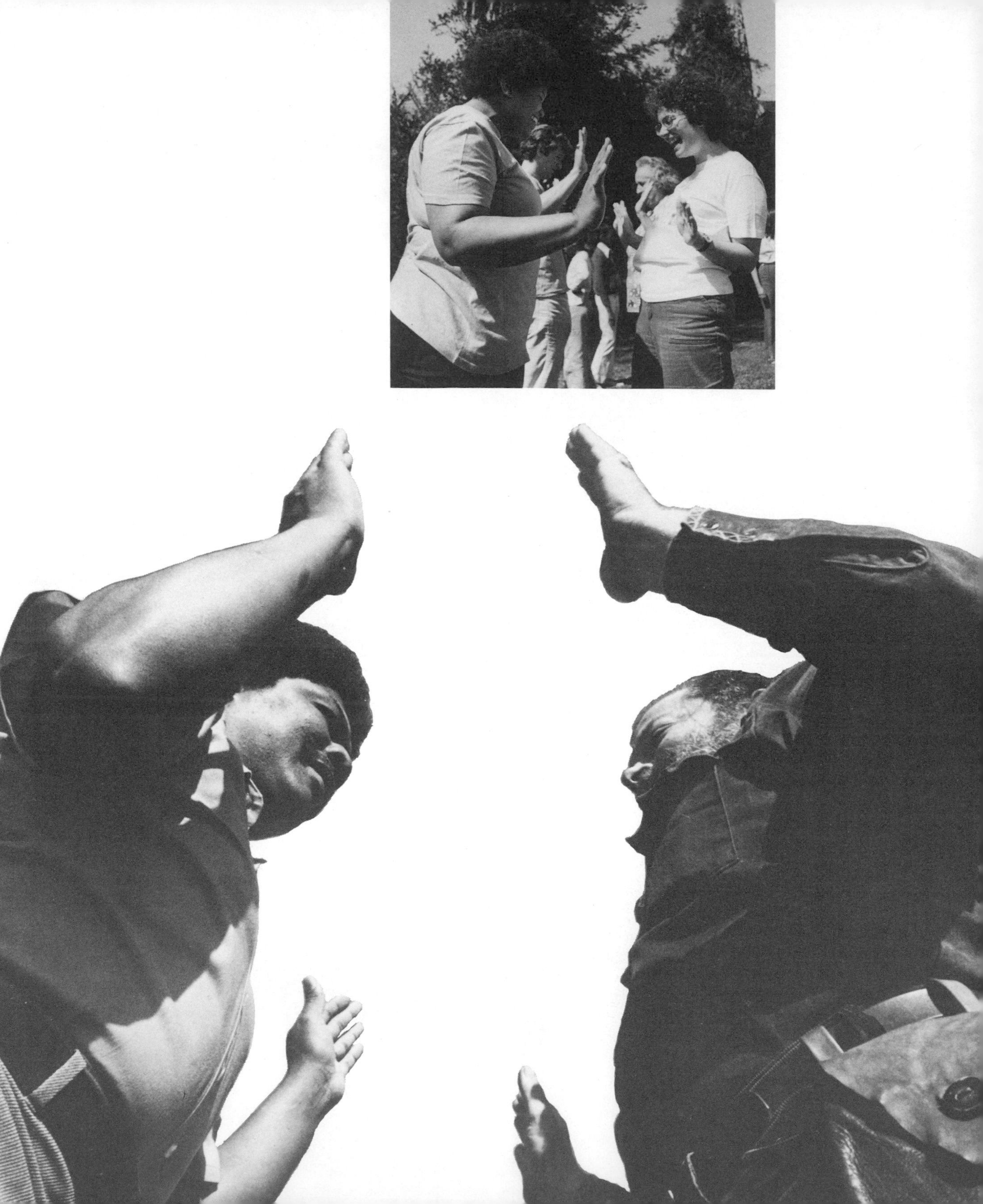

Stand-Off

This one-on-one battle for balance can be played almost anywhere at any time, and the only equipment needed is yourselves. The following rules and conventions for the game have been codified by Scott Beach, who is universally recognized as the Self-Proclaimed Intergalactic Champion of Stand-Off.

To play the game, two players stand face-to-face on a level surface at one arm's length. (If one player's arms are shorter or longer than the other's, split the difference.) The feet of each player must be side-by-side, smack together. The players present their hands with palms facing their partners. The object of Stand-Off is to cause your partner to lose balance, making contact with your hands *only*.

If your partner moves one or both feet while you retain your stance, you get one point. If he lunges forward and wraps himself around you in an impromptu *abrazzo*, that's also a point for you. If both of you lose balance, then neither gets a point. The game is won by the player who scores two out of three points.

It is permissible to dodge and feint with your hands, but at no time during the game may players make contact with any part of their partner's body other than the hands. If such contact is made, no penalties are imposed, but the offending player should reflect upon what's really going on.

Here's a version of Stand-Off inspired by the graceful martial art of aikido. The players start with their palms together and keep them in contact through each round. The object is still to make your partner lose balance, but no sudden moves are permissible. Played this way, the game becomes a beautiful slow-motion act that looks far more like a dance than a contest.

Note: A long session of Stand-Off can get your arms sore and leaden. Remember, you can always stop playing. Who needs sore and leaden arms? ■

Aura

Here's a one-on-one contest that's highly cooperative. You can't get it alone, but you can get it together.

Stand facing your partner at arms' length. Touch palms and close your eyes. Now feel the energy you are creating together.

Keeping your eyes closed, drop your hands and both turn around in place three times. Without opening your eyes, try to relocate your energy bodies by touching palms again.

This game always makes it as a spectator sport and is wildly contagious besides. Try playing it with your neighbor at the bus stop. (You might have to post a lookout, however, so that the bus doesn't rumble past a blissful group of commuters spinning on the curb.) ■

Frisbee Golf

Ever since the Frisbee made its appearance in the sports world twenty-odd years ago, people have been inventing new games by grafting Frisbees onto just about every traditional sport. We've tried Frisbee Football, Frisbee Baseball, even Frisbee Water Polo. Somehow, none of those games seem right. They all treat the Frisbee as just another ball.

It's not appropriate to inject the noble Frisbee into a game where you have to tolerate wobbling, slanting tosses and fight for its possession. A Frisbee is meant to soar gracefully, catch sunlight, dip with the wind, hover, and finally, at that unbelievable last moment, settle down gently at the end of its journey. There's only one sport that permits the Frisbee to express its full majesty: Frisbee Golf.

Pick a sunny Saturday morning, crisp, with dew still on the ground. Select your favorite Frisbee, call up a friend, and meet at the park for a round. Flip to see who gets to lay out the first hole. Choose an object a couple of hundred yards away for the pin—a tree, refuse can, or sprinkler head. Then map out the course—dog-legs, out-of-bounds, hazards. When you've both agreed on the layout of the first hole, you're ready to play it.

Your score will be the number of shots it takes to hit the object selected for the hole. Score by standard golf rules. After you've played the first hole, the other player gets to map out the next one. Be as inventive as you like, and play eighteen imaginative holes around your neighborhood.

You might have to come up with some special rules to deal with unusual qualities of the Frisbee itself. For instance, one feature of Frisbees is that people can't resist throwing them. Taking account of this, we've devised the Good Samaritan Rule. Basically, it provides that if a stranger good-naturedly picks up your Frisbee and tosses it back to you, you have to play your next shot from where the Frisbee lands. To ease the severity of this rule, you're allowed to try to catch your Good Samaritan's throw. If you succeed, you can play your shot over from where you make the catch, and you can deduct one point from your score.

The nice thing about Frisbee Golf is that there's never a greens' fee or a wait to tee off. You don't even *have* to yell "fore"—just be careful of your neighbor's prize tulips and hope your prized Master model doesn't fall into the jaws of a canine who's not likely to be a Good Samaritan. ■

Creating the Play Community

BERNIE DE KOVEN

Here we are, together, to have fun. We've already dispensed with the sense of any other purpose. We have no need to prove anything in particular to anyone in general. We're not looking to be therapized or taught or changed. We want to celebrate. We want to play.

We've got thousands of games to choose from. We don't feel that we have to play any special game in a special way. We're not together for that purpose. It's not a game that drew us to this place, it's the need, desire, inclination, instinct to share delight.

Some of our friends know games we've never heard of before. Their games may at first seem silly. It's hard to take them seriously. It's hard to feel that the games are important. It's easy to laugh, to laugh with. It's easy to play. The reward is in doing it. In rolling this absurdly big ball, pointlessly. In keeping it in the air. In lifting each other. In sitting in each other's laps. In pushing and pulling and running. In being tied together in a celebration of the fact that we are tied together. In quitting or joining for no reason.

It's not that their new games are especially important. It's that their games are new. No one is an expert lap sitter. No one is a professional ball pusher. So nobody has a reputation to risk. Nobody has anything to lose. If you enjoy yourself, you win.

Because the games are new, we get a sense that we're experimenting. No one guarantees anything. If a game doesn't work, we try to fix it, to see if we can make it work. After all, it's a new game. It's not official yet. In fact, we're the officials, all of us—the kids, the grandparents, everyone of us who has come to play. We make the judgments. We each take the responsibility for discovering what we can enjoy together. It makes so much more sense to change the game than to try to change the people who are there to play.

We are beginning to create a play community—not a forever community with a fixed code, but a temporary community with a code we make up as we go along, a community that we can continue creating anywhere, any time we find the people who want to create it with us.

The games we start with aren't competitive. (They could be played competitively if we wished, but not yet.) To establish the play community, we can't separate people into winners and losers. We can't begin with something that's going to divide us or measure us against each other. We begin the play community by embracing each other, by giving each person the opportunity to experience him- or herself as a full and equal member.

Later on, we might want to set up scoring systems. Sometimes scoring helps to focus on each other. It all depends on what we're scoring for. Suppose we decide to score ourselves as a team. We could give our team points for its teamness, for coordinating and balancing and giving each player full access to play. Suppose we score ourselves instead of each other. Suppose we divide up into teams, and each team decides what it would like the other team to give points for.

When we stand opposite each other in a game, it's not because we are, in fact, opposites. When we find ourselves on one particular side, it's not because we feel that one side is any better. We make the separation so that we can discover a new union.

The creation of a play community is remarkable to witness. It goes through many moods, through phases of coming together and scattering, of intensity and relaxation, of high and low times. For it to be whole, it must embrace all the modes of experiencing.

"Well, that game was a bummer." No blame. It just didn't feel good. Everybody splits. Walks around. Lies down. Hides. A few people sit to talk. Then they take turns talking. Then they start creating a fantasy. Then other people join. Then the fantasy becomes larger. More people join. People start moving, running around. New game. New high. Someone brings a parachute. Another new game. Then a mad run with everyone holding on, spinning across the field. Then exhaustion. Cloud watching. A sigh. A song. ■

Bernie De Koven, games designer and play facilitator, works with individuals and institutions to design games for their needs and help them integrate play with their lives. He founded and is associated with the Games Preserve (R.D. 1, Orchard Road, Fleetwood, Pennsylvania 19522), a twenty-five acre gathering place for people to experiment with and share play.

Games for a Dozen

VERY ACTIVE
Flying Dutchman
Catch the Dragon's Tail
Bola
Human Pinball
Go-Tag
Water Slide

ACTIVE
People Pyramids
Fox and Squirrel
Smaug's Jewels
Pieing
Stand Up
Ball Crawl

MODERATE
Knots
Red Handed
Lummi Sticks
Egg Toss
Rattlers
The Bone Game

Flying Dutchman

The name of this game conjures up visions of the legendary lost ship that endlessly roams the high seas in futile search of a port. Our human windjammers ultimately have better luck, but by the time they reach port, they are equally deserving of rest.

In our version, everyone but two players joins hands in a circle. The two who have been left out are the lost ship. Holding hands, they walk around the outside of the circle, seeking a port. When they decide upon a likely spot, they break the handhold of two people in the circle. Now the action begins.

At full tilt the lost ship has to navigate the circle one more time. Meanwhile, the two players whose hands were unjoined have to join hands again, start running around the outside of the circle in the opposite direction, and return to their port before the Flying Dutchman does. The first pair to make port closes the circle. The partners on the outside are left to roam in search of new harbors.

For variety, you might specify the mode of navigation to be hopping, jumping, running backwards, or piggyback. Or try making your way through a simulated fog—that is, close your eyes and grope your way into port. Take care midway 'round the circle, however. A crash encounter on the high seas could take the wind out of your sails. ■

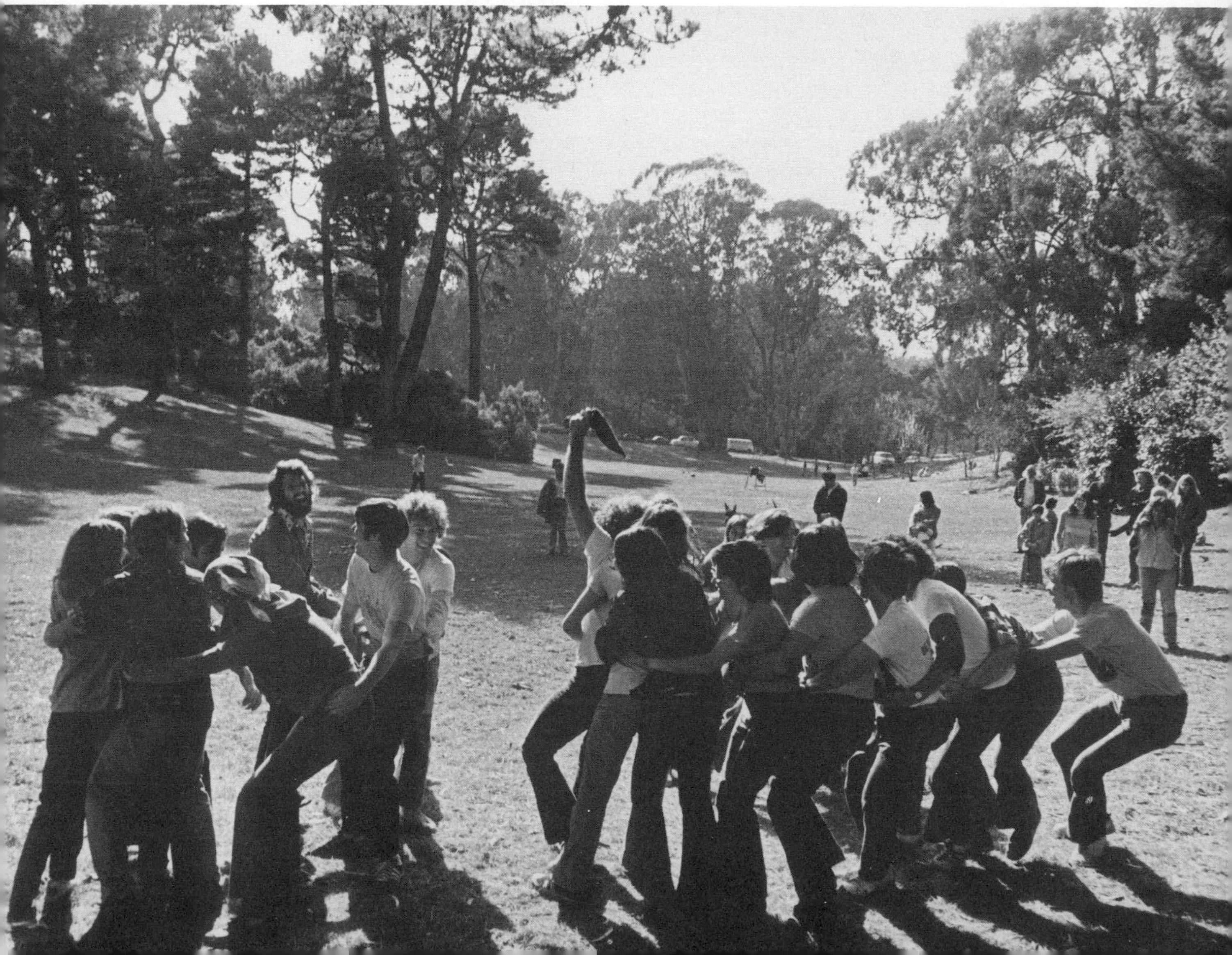

Catch the Dragon's Tail

It's one thing when a puppy chases its tail—and quite another when a dragon tries it. The difference you find here in tail is more than just a matter of scale.

You'll need a good-sized area for this event, clear of sudden pits and immovable oaks. About eight to ten people line up, one behind the other. Now, everyone puts their arms around the waist of the person in front of them. (You can't be ticklish around dragons.) The last person in line tucks a handkerchief in the back of his belt. To work up steam, the dragon might let out a few roars—fearsome enough, we wager, to put Hydra to shame.

At the signal, the dragon begins chasing its own tail, the object being for the person at the head of the line to snatch the handkerchief. The tricky part of this epic struggle is that the people at the front and the people at the end are clearly competing—but the folks in the middle aren't sure which way to go. When the head finally captures the tail, who's the defeated and who's the victor? Everyone! The head dons the handkerchief and becomes the new tail, while second from the front becomes the new head.

Two dragons trying to catch *each other's* tails is formidable—and also a great game. How about a whole field full of tail-chasing dragons? ■

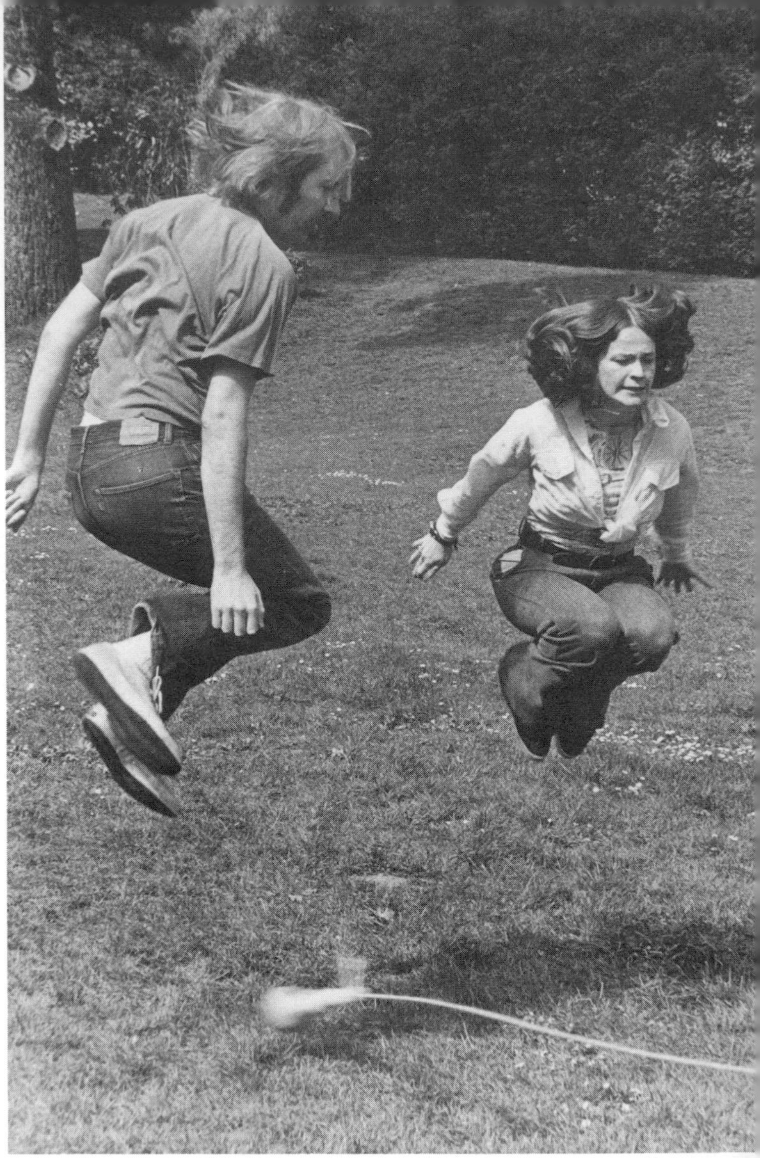

Bola

Down on the *pampas* of Argentina, gauchos use a *bola* to lasso their cattle. In the parks and fields of New Games events, we use it for a variety of jump rope. Like a lasso, the rope is twirled by one person. Everyone else leaps like calves on the run.

To make a Bola, stuff a rubber softball into a long sock and tie a knot in the sock just above the ball. (You have also just made a Schmerltz. Turn back to page 27.) Now tie a clothesline rope securely to the sock. Lie down on your back and start spinning the Bola, slowly letting out the rope.

When you've got it rotating at a radius of about 12 feet, everyone can begin jumping into the circle. After a few trips and spills for practice, jumpers will be ready for some stepped-up action. Increase the speed of the Bola until it's really zinging. As jumpers get a little more agile, they might try skipping the rope hand-in-hand with a partner. Or how about everyone holding hands?

If you're nicked by the Bola, you might find yourself tied up at the ankles and hitting the dust with all the grace of a bull on the pampas. But don't worry; no one will brand you as hopelessly clumsy. Just pick yourself up and take another crack at it. ■

Human Pinball

Here's your chance to be a flipper in a giant pinball machine. (Your dream come true.) The lights and bells may be missing on our organic model, but there's plenty of action.

All players except one stand in a circle, facing *outwards*. Spread your legs as wide as comfortable until your feet are touching your neighbors' on either side. Everyone bend down and swing your arms between your legs. This is what it feels like to be a flipper.

The one non-flipper enters the circle as the movable target. The flippers try to hit him by knocking a volleyball or rubber playground ball back and forth across the circle. Whoever hits the target gets one point and also gets to be the new target. Every time the ball goes out of the circle, the target scores a point. (However, the target's only job is to *avoid* the ball. Only flippers can flip it.)

Exactly what these points are good for is questionable, since everyone is entitled to as many "Free Games" as they want. And considering the circumstances, it's far more likely that the rushing blood would swell your head long before any phenomenal score could. Maybe that's why no one yet claims to be the World's Human Pinball Wizard. ■

Go-Tag

This is a version of a game that's played with intense seriousness in India and Pakistan. You can enjoy it at whatever skill and strategy level you decide to play.

Everyone squats in a line, alternate players facing opposite directions. (Check the photo below to make sure you're set up correctly.) If you think of the line as the central axis, you can imagine an oval track running around the line. (There's no need to mark boundaries; the track is defined by the axis.)

The person at one end of the line will be the first runner. He may run around the track in either direction. The person at the other end will be the first chaser. She may start running either clockwise or counter-clockwise, but she may not switch directions once she starts. The object of the game is for the chaser to tag the runner.

What keeps this from becoming just a steeplechase game of tag is that the chaser works with the other people squatting in the line. As she is chasing around the track, she can tap the *back* of any squatting player and shout, "Go!" The tapped player steps forward to begin the chase, while the old chaser replaces him, squatting in the line. This maneuver is called the "Go-Tag," and makes the chaser a group entity, able to cross over the center of the line and change the direction of the chase.

When you first play the game, practice the Go-Tag maneuver a few times so that everyone understands how it works. Then start playing more seriously, exploring the strategies that the chasers can use. The key to this game is to change chasers frequently and rapidly enough to catch the runner off guard. Running speed is not as important as reflexes and quick thinking.

When the runner is finally tagged, he squats at one end of the line, the person who tagged him becomes the new runner, and the person at the other end of the line becomes the starting chaser for the next round. ■

Water Slide

Suppose someone were to spread a long plastic sheet on the ground and spray it with a hose. Would *you* be ready to take a running slide?

This is where all pretentions, egos, and dry concerns get abandoned. Scrap your pride. Take a ride on the Water Slide! ■

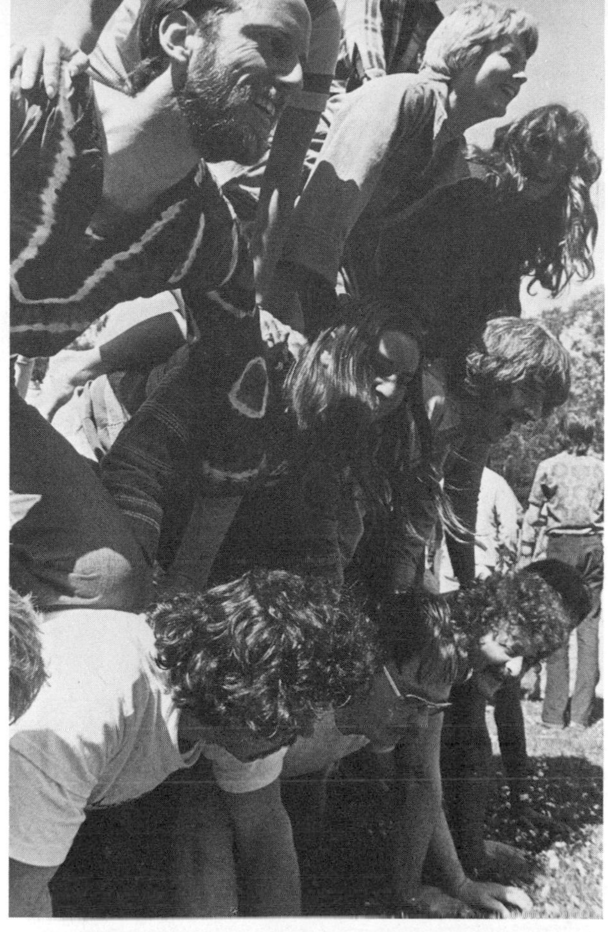

People Pyramids

It took 2,600,000 stone blocks to build the Great Pyramid at Gizeh. Our sights aren't set quite so high, but our pyramids are really great. They're built of people—and you only need ten of them.

Start with four stout-hearted hulks on the bottom. Get three mid-sized, inner-directed types on the next level, and two, small courageous acrobats above them. Top it all off with one very light, expendable child. This is called the Hot Fudge Sundae Model.

The Big Rock Candy Mountain Model features a circular base and lots more people. In Spain, where they've been building these for over two centuries, this one is called a *castell*. Sometimes these Castillian castles reach nine levels high—crowned, no doubt, by a child trained in mountain climbing. We wouldn't recommend such heights unless you invent a New Game called the Parachute-People Catch. ■

Fox and Squirrel

This is one of those wonderful games in which you can't tell who's playing with or against whom. While it's not very demanding physically, it somehow always manages to be played at near-panic level.

You'll need three balls. Two of them should be similar—for the foxes—and the other, perhaps smaller and distinctly different, for the squirrel. The object of the game is for the foxes to catch the squirrel by tagging whoever is holding the squirrel ball with one (or both) of the fox balls. If two against one seems unfair, just wait. You'll find out how foxy squirrels can be.

Everyone stands in a circle and begins passing the fox balls from player to player. With a bit of practice, you should be able to get them all moving at top speed. Try out a few sudden sly reversals as well.

Now here's the tricky-squirrel bit. We all know that foxes are quick, but squirrels are slick—and able to leap besides. That means you can only *pass* the foxes to the player next to you, but you can *throw* the squirrel across the circle. To keep everyone alert, call out "Fox" or "Squirrel" each time you pass one of the balls. (The bedlam will certainly dispel any illusion of the forest.)

While there may be that tendency, the squirrel isn't *always* the favored underdog. You might detect the fox sympathizers by noticing who tosses the squirrel your way just as two foxes are converging on you. ■

Smaug's Jewels

"My armour is like tenfold shields, my teeth are swords, my claws spears, the shock of my tail a thunderbolt, my wings a hurricane, and my breath death!" brags the dragon Smaug to Bilbo Baggins. In Tolkein's fantasy, *The Hobbit*, Bilbo had come to raid Smaug's priceless horde of gold and jewels. In our version of the story, the stakes may not be as high nor the dragon so formidable, but the game is basically the same—to avoid the deadly touch of the dragon and to snatch his treasure.

One person chosen as Smaug stands guard over his jewels. (A handkerchief placed on the ground is a less glamorous but eminently more practical substitute.) Everyone else forms a circle around him and tries to steal the treasure without being tagged. A good roar and some fancy footwork on the part of the dragon can be nearly as impressive as death breath and thunderbolt tails.

Smaug the Mighty can range as far from his jewels as he dares. If you get touched by him, you are instantly frozen in place until the end of the game. But don't worry—it's a rare dragon that reigns for more than thirty seconds.

A popular strategy for treasure-snatching is to sneak up behind and reach between the dragon's legs to grab the jewels. Or if you make believe you're frozen, you might catch Smaug unawares. And then there's always the mass charge where most get sacrificed but one gets the treasure. This at least gives everyone the opportunity to confront a new dragon, for the old one is replaced by the treasure snatcher.

If by chance Smaug manages to get everyone before they get his jewels, he has the option to leave you all frozen, solid as bones, for the next 500 years. Dragons are not known for mercy. ■

Pieing

Although pie-fighting has been officially outlawed in most civilized countries, it has never been totally suppressed. You'll still find underground Pieings being held in out-of-the-way farmyards and abandoned garages. The following rules, adapted from those formulated by Jack J. Anderson (the Marquis of Queensbury of the pie-fighting world), are now the accepted standard for all Pieings in North America west of the Rocky Mountains:

The Match. A *Pieing* shall consist of three rounds, called *Pannings*.

Playing Area. The playing area, called the *Pie-R-Square*, shall be a circle ten feet in diameter and divided into halves, called *Piepieces*. Except in times of drought, the Pie-R-Square should be located on a grassy area.

Equipment. Regulation equipment shall consist of lightweight paper plates, whipped cream, and absorbant Turkish towels. (There is a proposal presently under consideration by the Rules Committee to suspend the use of aerosol-propelled whipped cream.)

Contestants. There shall be two contestants, called *Pieplayers*, at each Panning. They may compete in uniforms of their choice, but no immodest dress is permitted. Each Pieplayer may have one assistant, called a *Second-Helping*, who shall prepare each Pieplayer's pies and administer rejuvenescent towellings between Pannings. The Second-Helpings must remain outside the Pie-R-Square and behind their Pieplayer's Piepieces.

Officials. A pieing shall be officiated by a Referee and two Judges, each of whom shall score the match. The Referee shall also call fouls, and is the only official who may dare enter the playing area.

Competition. Each Panning commences when the Pieplayers enter their respective Piepieces, each with pie in open hand, and call "Ready, Whip." During each Panning, the Pieplayers must stay within the Pie-R-Square and may physically contact their opponent only with their pies.

Fouls. A foul occurs when (1) a Pieplayer steps out of the Pie-R-Square; (2) action begins without both Pieplayers calling out "Ready, Whip"; (3) a Pieplayer holds a pie with other than an open hand; (4) Pieplayers make contact other than with their pies; (5) a Pieplayer is guilty of unpieperson like conduct. If a foul takes place, the Referee calls "No Pie," stops the action, and pieplay begins with a new Panning.

Scoring. *Piepoints* are awarded after each Panning as follows: a *Splat* is worth 10 Piepoints; a *Sploosh*, 7 to 9 points; a *Slurp*, 4 to 6 points; a *Slop*, 1 to 3 points. No Piepoints are awarded (or deducted) for inadvertantly Splooshing the Referee.

End of Match. After three Pannings, the Piepoints are totalled and the Pieplayer with the most Piepoints is declared the winner. Any Pieplayer who wins three sanctioned Pieings enters the ranks of the *Upper Crust* and is entitled to participate in the Big Meringue. ■

Stand Up

This cooperative game is one of our favorites for getting a New Games group together. You can start with just one friend and end up with a whole crowd of struggling, stumbling, giggling humanity.

Sit on the ground, back-to-back with your partner, knees bent and elbows linked. Now simply stand up together. With a bit of cooperation and a little practice, this shouldn't be too hard.

By the time you've got this mastered, you'll probably have drawn an interested spectator. Have her join you on the ground, and all three try to stand up. This feat should take you just long enough to attract another onlooker. Have him join you. Four people standing up together might be a genuine accomplishment.

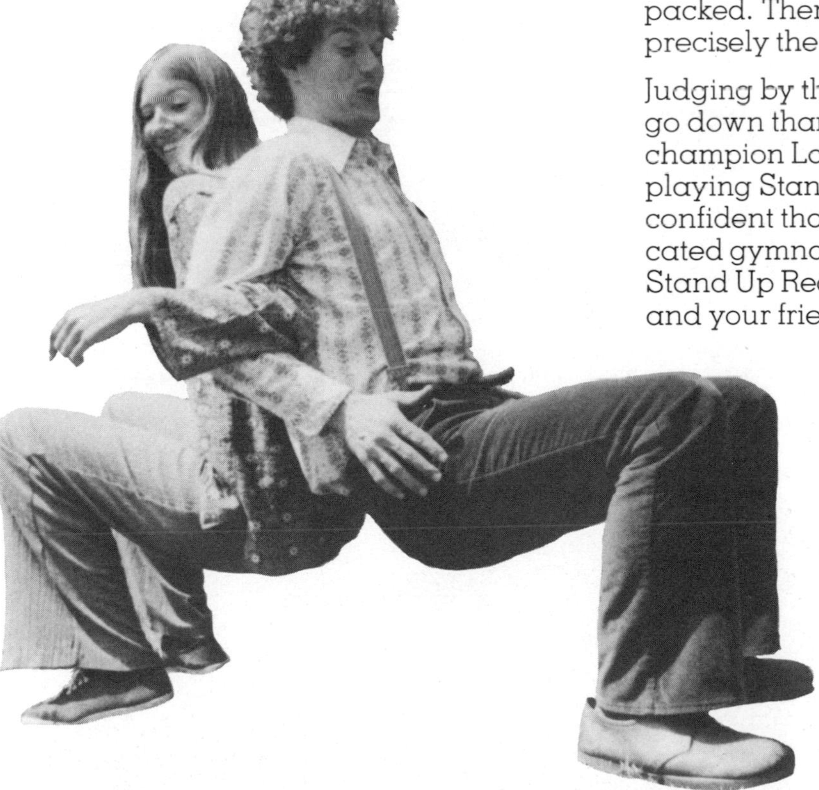

By this time you should realize that there's more struggling, stumbling, and giggling each time you add another person. But this very fact assures you of an endless supply of fascinated spectators, ready to join up to help you get off the ground.

A gracefully executed Mass Stand Up (any number greater than five) is like a blossoming flower—but a more rare event. To achieve it, start by sitting close and firmly packed. Then all stand up quickly and at precisely the same moment.

Judging by the records, it must be easier to go down than up. Can you imagine 1,468 champion Lap Sitters in Palos Verdes playing Stand Up together? However, we're confident that somewhere a group of dedicated gymnasts is practicing for the World Stand Up Record. Write us if you think you and your friends have made it. ■

PLAY HARD.

Ball Crawl

Maybe it's a basic human drive for ascension, or simply the wish to be "sitting on top of the world." Whatever the reason, just leave an Earthball unattended in a public place and people will invariably try to climb on it. Those who succeed will invariably try to keep from falling off.

Once you're up, maybe you can make the Earth turn by crawling across its surface. Romp across continents and leap over oceans as if they were puddles. Realize your boldest dreams! ■

Knots

Knots is a game that gets people together by getting them apart. About a dozen players can tie on a good one.

To form the knot, stand in a circle, shoulder-to-shoulder, and place your hands in the center. Now everybody grab a couple of hands. If you ever want to get out of this, make sure that no one holds both hands with the same person or holds the hand of a person right next to them. It might take a bit of switching around to get the knot tied right. (If you have too much trouble getting this part together, you might want to quit before you try getting it apart!)

Now comes the true test. You'll probably notice that there are two basic approaches to untangling the knot. The Activists dive right into the problem—under, over, and through their teammates—hoping they'll hit upon the solution. Instead, they might well hit upon one of the Analysts, firmly rooted, hands locked in a dignified tableau, carefully surveying the situation before instructing each player precisely where to move and in what order.

Since you're all in the same tangle together, you'll have to come to some agreement as to which approach to follow. (Note: pivoting on your handholds without actually breaking your grip will add a lot of grace and eliminate the need for a chiropractor.) When at last the knot is unraveled (hurrah!), you will find yourselves in one large circle or, occasionally, two interconnected ones (amazing!).

Every once in a while an Analyst will discover the one tangle which prevents the knot from resolving itself. At this point, no other remedy being possible, an Activist can administer emergency "knot-aid" (a momentary break in hands) so you can get on to the next game. ■

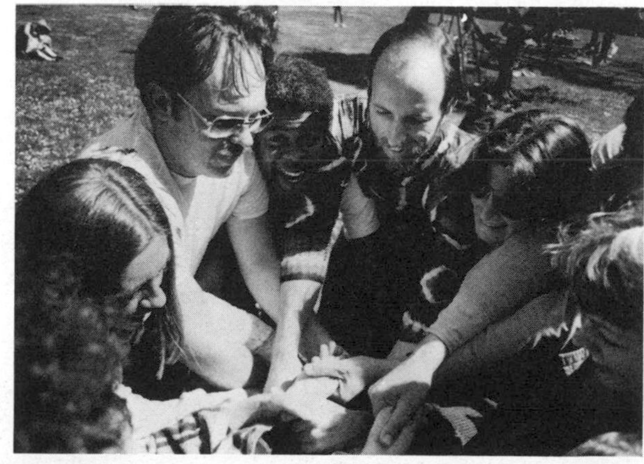

Red Handed

Here's a legitimate chance to see how sneaky you can be. And the only consequence if you get caught is having to catch someone who might be even sneakier.

Everyone forms a circle, and one person, chosen as IT, stands in the center. While IT closes her eyes, the other players pass a small object (like a marble or a stone) from person to person.

The sneakiest method of passing is to hold the marble in one fist, palm down, and drop it into the palm-up hand of the next person. Then he passes it from one fist to the other and on. With a little practice, you'll be able to accomplish a quick and sneaky pass without even looking.

IT signals and opens her eyes. Who among all these innocent-looking people has the marble? If she detects a suspicious look on someone's face, she walks up and taps one of his fists. If he's empty-handed, she moves on. Meanwhile everyone has been passing the marble around, virtually under IT's nose. (Fake passes, as decoys, by people who don't have the marble are an integral part of the game.)

If you have the marble and IT catches your eye, she may soon catch more than that unless you can pull a good angel face. If she sees through that to the sneaky devil beneath, you've been caught "Red-Handed." Congratulations! You're the new IT. ■

Lummi Sticks

War, for the gentle New Zealand Maori, is a highly refined art. In World War II, during an encounter between the British and the Maori, the British lieutenant reportedly was forced to hoist a white flag and declare that his troops were unable to continue for lack of ammunition. In the true spirit of fair play, the Maori chieftain replied, "Then we'll give you half of ours," and the game continued.

While Lummi Sticks apparently has very little to do with combat, you might recognize that same Maori sense of style and cooperation in this game, also invented by them. The key element is rhythm, and its variations are traditionally set against the background of a flowing chant.

You can play with any number of players, from two on up. Everyone holds a pair of Lummi Sticks vertically, one in each hand. We use wooden dowels, one inch in diameter and four feet long, but you can choose to play with any size stick, from one to four feet. (Just make sure they're all the same length.)

Facing your partner, you both begin to beat a slow rhythm with your sticks, tapping either end on the ground, table, or floor. Once the whole group has established the rhythm, you can begin adding variations. Until you're really expert, it works best for everyone to do the same pattern at the same time.

Maintaining the rhythm, click your two sticks together every few beats. Then, between touching them to the ground, click one or both of them against your partner's sticks or your neighbors' on either side. Try various combinations of all these. As you develop dexterity, you can begin tossing sticks through the air to each other in time with the rhythm.

Among the Maori, there are many traditional patterns for the game, beginning with simple forms and progressing to very complex ones. As you play, you will discover your own patterns. The important thing is to maintain the rhythm, let it carry you, speed up the tempo or slow it down as suits the group, and develop variations as the spirit moves you.

The chant is an important part of the game. Musical notation and words for the traditional Maori chant can be found in resource books, but the game will be new as you invent your own or adapt any short rhythmical song you know. Repeat the song a certain number of times for each pattern you create. Chanting holds the action together and gives it order, as well as influencing the atmosphere of the game.

Painting, carving, or wood-burning designs on your Lummi Sticks can be a beautiful preparation or interlude for the game. Why not set up a Lummi Sticks jam session in your neighborhood and have everyone begin by making their own unique pair of sticks? ■

Egg Toss

Here's a way to experience the thrill and excitement of an egg toss without splaying tomorrow's soufflé across the grass—or your shirt. You'll need a bunch of small balloons filled with water—not too much, not too little. (You should feel a little trepidation when you hold the shivering mass.)

Everybody choose a sturdy-looking water balloon and a partner and form two lines, facing each other, about three fee apart. At the signal—thinking air—toss the balloon gingerly to your partner, who should try to catch it even more gingerly. End round one. No showers yet.

After each round, everyone take a step backwards and throw again. If the balloon doesn't manage to drench you when it bursts, at least it puts you out of the game. If you do get soaked, you might want to share that with your partner by giving her a big hug.

The last two to keep their balloon afloat are obviously the winners and may dispose of that last gurgling orb as they see fit. ■

Rattlers

At close of day, many a cowpoke has spun out his yarn of being "higher than a kite on a rattlesnake bite." Well, here's the foundation for your own high time with the rattlers.

Everyone forms a circle around two players. They are both blindfolded and given a rattle (tin cans and pebbles make good ones). One is going to try to tag the other. The rattlers enter the snake pit, and the game begins.

To get a fix on each other's positions, either rattler may shake his rattle at any time, and the other must immediately respond by shaking hers. However, the pursuer is allowed to initiate only five shakes to locate his quarry, while the pursued can rattle away as much as she dares.

While making sure that neither of the rattlers wanders out of the snake pit, the other players also participate by helping the pursuer keep count of his shakes and cheering and shouting things charming to snakes. To make the game even more interesting, and to keep the other players from feeling like spectators, why not let them move around, thereby changing the size and shape of the snake pit?

What's the best Rattler strategy? Do you strike fast, or hunt slow and easy? Do you steal about silently, or lead your pursuer on a wild snake chase? We leave it to you, but you might remember that rattlers are seldom known to attack unless they're approached first—except in August, when they're a bit itchy before shedding their skins. But that's another game (see page 119). ■

The Bone Game

Versions of this game of chance have been found among 81 North American Indian tribes from Oklahoma to Alaska. Because the game depends solely upon gesture, it was easily played by people who did not share a common spoken language.

Unlike many of our New Games, which tend to be boisterous, the traditional tenor of this one is solemn and intense. To encourage this spirit, the game should be played in a peaceful setting. Among the Wichita, the game was opened with an invocation to the Sun, asking that the event might be quiet and orderly, that the losing side would not resent the winners, and that everyone might be happy at the close of the game. A perfect New Game!

To play, you need four bones or round sticks, each small enough to be concealed in your closed fists. Two of the bones are marked by wrapping a thong or thread around them. The other two are left unmarked.

The players, in two tribes of about five people each, sit or kneel in lines, facing each other. Each tribe has a set of ten sticks to use as counters. Traditionally, these were arrows to be thrust into the ground at each scoring. The game will end when one tribe has captured all the counters.

One tribe chooses two people to play as hiders. They sit in the center of their tribe's line, each hider concealing in his or her fists two of the bones, one marked and one unmarked. The other tribe chooses a shooter, who will try to guess where the marked bones are.

Both tribes begin swaying and chanting. (Versions of the traditional chant are recorded in books on the games of North American Indians, but part of the game is inventing your own.) The chant unites the players, growing and fading, quickening or slowing down, according to the mood of the game. The chant is a vital part of the game, for the contest is not merely between the hiders and the shooter, but between the spirits of the two tribes.

The shooter kneels before the two hiders and begins to test them by showing a series of hand gestures which indicate the four possible ways in which the bones they hold might be arranged:

Palm down—the marked bones are in the two *outside fists* of the hiders.

Hand on edge—the marked bones are in the two *inside fists*.

Thumb pointing left (closed fist)—the marked bones are in each of the two fists on the *left side*.

Thumb pointing right—the marked bones are in each of the two *right fists*.

The hiders look straight ahead, along with the rest of their tribe, trying not to reveal the position of the bones. The shooter, meanwhile, searches for any glance or gesture that might give them away. When the shooter feels he knows where the bones are, he shouts, "Ho!" and shoots out one of the hand signals. The hiders open their fists to reveal the marked bones.

If the shooter correctly guesses the position of both marked bones, his tribe takes the bones and chooses two hiders, and the other tribe chooses a shooter. If the shooter's guess has missed both bones, he gives up two of his tribe's counter sticks to the other side and continues shooting.

The shooter's signal might locate only one of the marked bones. (For example, if the bones are concealed in the hiders' two outside fists, and the shooter gestures with his thumb to the right, he has located only one bone.) In this case, the shooter takes the one marked bone from its hider and forfeits one of his tribe's counters for the incorrect guess. The remaining bone is once again hidden among the two hiders and the shooter guesses again. For each subsequent guess that is incorrect, the shooter's tribe must give up another counter.

When the shooter succeeds in capturing both marked bones, his tribe becomes the hiders. (Shooters and hiders may be changed only between rounds.) This game of chanting and guessing has been known to go for hours, even days, without the players growing weary.

The Native Americans placed great meaning in the Bone Game. They did not think of luck as most of us do. For them, it manifested power, and was an expression of the energy underlying all of life. ■

REFEREE

The Player-Referee's Non-Rulebook

There are three ways to referee a New Game. The most traditional way is in the role of an official. The Official-Referee walks onto the center of a field and announces, "All right, we're going to play Catch the Dragon's Tail. Everyone form lines of eight players and each player lock his arms around the person in front of him." The Official-Referee's job is to make sure that all the players follow his instructions.

You can also referee as a coach. The Coach-Referee takes eight players in hand and says, "Here, you put your arms around this person; you get behind her, like this; and you stand at the end of the line, like this." The Coach-Referee helps the players play the game.

The third way to referee New Games is to put your arms around someone's waist, look over your shoulder, and say, "Come over here and put your arms around my waist!"

Although there's room for all three kinds of refereeing in New Games, they work best when each player is a referee—when everyone assumes responsibility for the game and for the other players. What follows is a guide to becoming a Player-Referee, but it's not a directive. The Player-Referee has only one rule to follow: "Play Hard, Play Fair, Nobody Hurt." All the rest of New Games is improvisation.

The First Game. *The easiest way to get New Games going is to start playing one. If you're having fun, others will want to join you. Stand Up is a great game for starters because you don't need a lot of people to begin, and the game naturally draws people into it as it progresses. Knots is another good game for openers because you can get the players involved in the game without having to explain it to them. First arrange ten people holding hands, then tell them that the point of the game is to get untangled. In Knots, no one can leave the game without destroying it. Once people are committed, they'll play, and they'll discover that the games you're playing are fun.*

Start with games that don't immediately exclude people because of too much activity or special skill requirements. Some people will shy away from Stand-Off because they're afraid they're going to lose. Start playing Aura with them. Once you've made contact in a game based on shared purpose, your partner will be more likely to trust you in a competitive one.

If you have a large group of people on hand, start with games that will get them physically in touch with each other and cooperating, like People Pass or Caterpillar. These games help create the atmosphere of community that's essential when you're playing New Games with many people. People Pyramids is perfect for building a play community because it requires players of all sizes to make the pyramid work.

Even if you're starting with a group that wants to play more active games, start with ones that don't require a lot of explanation and in which there's always room for others to join, such as Smaug's Jewels or Bola. And keep an eye out for spectators. Most people who stand around watching a game really want to be playing with you. Invite them. If the game you're playing isn't suitable for their physical abilities, try to change the game so that they'll feel free to play.

Energy. *One of the important roles of the Player-Referee is to stay aware of the play energy and help direct it, but first it has to be built. You can't jump right into the most active games. Have everyone get involved in a moderately physical game like Bug Tug before going all out in an active game like British Bulldog. If you try to play too many active games in succession, even the most hardy players will eventually get exhausted and the built up energy will be dissipated. Let everyone catch their breath while you play a game like Pina. By varying the activity level of the games, you'll be able to keep everyone fresh and energetic.*

The play energy is also affected by the quality of the game and the extent to which it ties the group together. A game like Snake-in-the-Grass doesn't build much group awareness because each player is free to express himself individually. This is true as

well of a minimally active game like Vampire. On the other hand, some games naturally bind people together—again regardless of whether they're active, like Blob and Amoeba Race, or passive, like Prui and Ooh-Ahh. Certain games, like the Mating Game, will work best when everyone is in an exuberant mood. The individually expressive games build energy, but the group awareness games help preserve it. Interspersing the games that offer individual and group play is a way of keeping everyone spirited, but still playing together.

You can also maintain the group's play energy simply by keeping everyone involved in the game. Let each game run its natural course, but change to a new one before the players lose their enthusiasm for it. Before explaining the rules of a new game, have the players stand in the configuration in which the game will be played. Not only is it much easier to understand the rules for Flying Dutchman when everyone's holding hands in a circle and two people are marching around the outside—the players are also being made part of the game as it's being explained. For the same reason, it's better not to play a game so that players are eliminated. Instead, have captured or tagged players switch sides, as we do in Rock/Paper/Scissors.

There are no hard and fast rules for managing what we've called the play energy, but it's important to recognize that New Games runs on it. If you are able to perceive this energy and tailor the games around it, all the players will feel that New Games is a celebrative experience.

Creativity. *The descriptions of the games in this book don't read like a rule book. We wanted to convey the concept and spirit behind each game, but we didn't want to give the impression that there is a right way to play any of them. The games presented here are a starting point for your own exploration into play. Adapt them to your needs and tastes. Make the games your own.*

By changing the rules, you can determine just how difficult it will be to "win" the game. For example, if everyone's having trouble finding the marble in Red Handed, rule that the tapped player has to show both hands instead of one, or have two marbles going around the circle. This will add a bit of luck to the game, on IT's behalf.

You can radically alter the nature of a game by changing the equipment used. Try playing Fox and Squirrel with Frisbees, or Fraha with your bare hands and a tennis ball. You can also create a whole new game around a piece of equipment. One afternoon, we devised a team game for Schmerltz, played somewhat like lacrosse and based on the rule that when you catch the Schmerltz, you have to keep it spinning while holding the tail and have to throw it again on the third spin.

If you find that some part of a game is dull for you, invent a rule to take care of that. We needed a circle of people in Rattlers to keep the blindfolded players from wandering off, but everyone got bored just standing around being nothing more than a barrier. Then we thought of letting the spectators change the shape of the snake pit, thus making them part of the game and giving the game itself a new dimension.

You can easily make a game new by changing the number of people playing it. Catch the Dragon's Tail played with one eight-person dragon becomes a very different game when you have two dragons chasing each other's tails. One day we played with four dragons, and came up with the rule that each time one dragon catches another's tail, the two dragons join into one long dragon. New game.

You can start with an idea from an old game and follow it wherever it takes you. That's how most of the games in this book evolved. If you're going to invent a new game, try changing or devising one rule at a time. Play the game that way for a bit, then look for the least

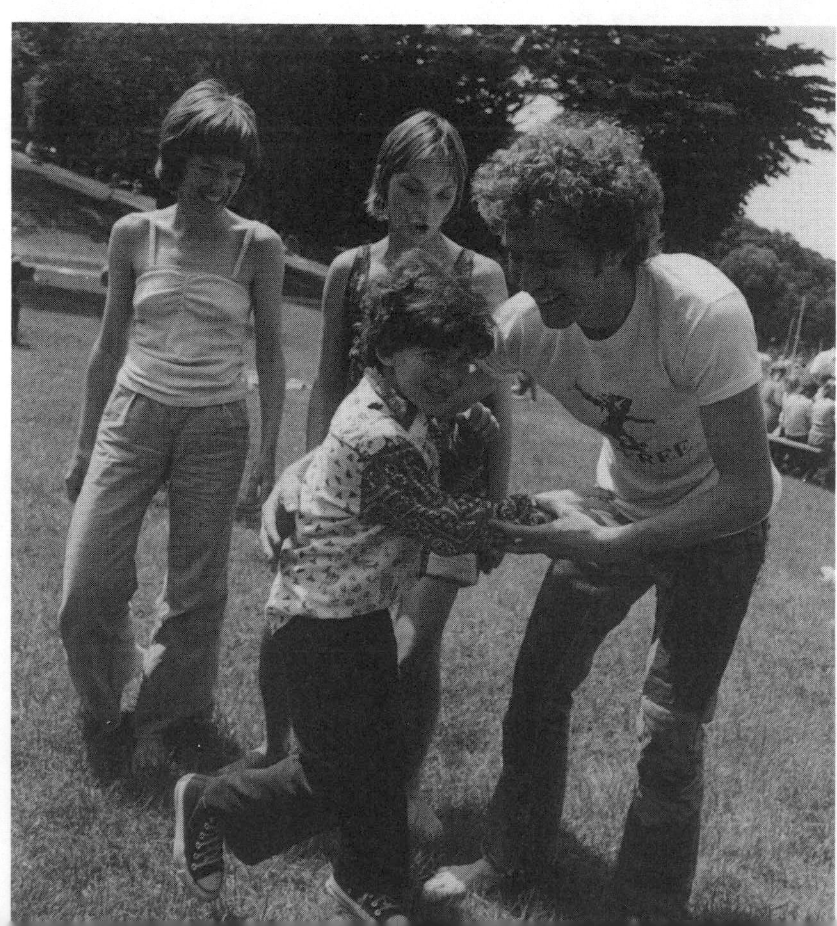

exciting part of that game and make a rule to correct that. Keep going, and soon you'll have a completely new game. (For some insights on what makes a game a good one, see Stewart Brand's article on page 137.) And never be afraid to fall back on an old favorite if you decide that the game you've been experimenting with isn't working.

Safety. The most important consideration of the Player-Referee has to be the safety of everyone playing the game. Make sure that the area you have chosen to play in is free of hazards such as glass, rocks, or holes, and don't let players wear hard-soled shoes if you're planning on playing active games. Most importantly, make sure that the games are suitable for all the players. Don't suggest a Clench a Wench relay race for people not used to strenuous activity.

If you're playing a game that involves physical impact, be certain that the players can handle it. You can reduce the level of activity or impact by changing the design of the game. For example, in Dho-Dho-Dho it should be stipulated that no one can be grabbed below the waist. If you need to make the game even less active, restrict the time during which impact is allowed by permitting the dho-dho to be grabbed only after she has tagged someone on the other team.

It's crucial that every player be his own referee with regard to safety. Each player must understand that he can play "all out" only if it won't endanger the other players, and only if all the players are prepared to play that way. Before playing a potentially rough game like Slaughter or British Bulldog, explain that restraint is as much a part of the game as is action, and that each player should gauge his force to match that of his opponent, not overwhelm him.

The greatest safety problems seem to arise when there is a very wide range of size, strength, and skill among the players in the game. If there are smaller people playing, it's important that everyone be aware of them before the game begins. Some players will nevertheless get caught up in the game and start playing too rough. Look out for this and point it out to anyone who's getting so carried away with the game that he's forgetting about the people. It's vital to the success of New Games that everyone feel confident that they can play in a safe and supportive environment.

Competition. Many people think of New Games as non-competitive. Of course this isn't the case. Most of the games in this book involve competition—it's what gives New Games its vitality. In fact, what distinguishes New Games from traditional sports is the value placed on true competition and the effort made to foster it.

Bernie De Koven has pointed out that the structure of every game is based on a goal and a resistance against achieving it. The effort each player makes to overcome the resistance and achieve the goal is the heart of the game and what makes it enjoyable and gratifying. In most games, the resistance is supplied by your opponent trying to achieve her goal. Your opponent is therefore your partner in the game. The best games are those in which you can play your hardest and

still count on your opponent to meet your effort—to compete with you.

In New Games, we try to keep each game competitive by making sure that everyone is evenly matched, or at least playing to the same end. If you're playing with people of mixed abilities, have the better players team with the less skillful ones, as in Siamese Soccer. In Rock/Paper/Scissors, have the faster runners face off against each other. When you play Slaughter, give the stronger players a handicap by having them play with one hand behind their backs. They'll enjoy the game much more playing that way than if they were easily able to overpower their opponents. Tug of War is a good game only so long as neither side wins.

If you do have a group of evenly matched players, some of the games in this book can provide opportunity for heated competition. We described how Skin the Snake can be turned into a demanding field event. Dho-Dho-Dho is played in martial arts training, and a version of Go-Tag is played very competitively in India and Pakistan. Hunker Hawser and Stand-Off place a premium on skill and awareness. The Bone Game is played very intensely by the American Indians. Even a non-competitive exercise like Lummi Sticks affords endless possibilities for coordinated group effort. It's fine to play New Games with an eye to skill and excellence, but be sure that all the players agree on how seriously they're going to play the game.

The Player-Referee values competition, but places no importance on winning. No one keeps track of the results of New Games. No one remembers, or cares, who was the last person out in Islands, or whether someone was IT in Hug Tag. If there's no premium placed on being the winner, then no one has to worry about being a loser. The only measure of success in New Games is whether everyone had fun playing.

Teams. Many New Games involve dividing into teams, but as with competition, teams are solely a means of enjoying the game. They're created for the moment, not as a way of identifying the winners or losers.

Make sure that there are different teams for each game and choose teams at random. Have people born on odd-numbered

days play against those with even-numbered birthdays. Divide people according to odd- or even-numbered ages, or split the alphabet and have people join teams according to the letters of their first or last names.

Be creative. You can even make a game out of joining into teams. Have everyone close their eyes; then walk among the players whispering "Duck" or "Cow" into the ears of alternate people. When everyone has been assigned an animal, set them loose to find their teammates with their eyes still closed, aided only by the quacking or mooing sounds they can make. By the time everyone finally gets together, the Ducks and Cows will be eager to take each other on in a spirited game of Slaughter. And no one had to be the last chosen.

If you're going to be playing with a very large group of people unfamiliar with New Games, you might find it helpful to organize the referees into a team. Have one referee function as the official, setting up and explaining the game, while other referees help as coaches and players. If you do referee in teams, make sure that you share the three roles so that no one gets stuck just officiating.

The key to playing New Games is realizing that there's only one team. The officials, coaches, players, Ducks, Cows, partners, and opponents are all playing on the same side. When everyone plays that way, everyone is sure to win.

The Last Game. *Your day of playing New Games should end so that everyone leaves* with high spirits and a sense of shared experience. It's good for people to be joyously tired by the end of the day, but don't play so long that the games die as players slip away exhausted. Try to sense the mood of the group and end while people are still enjoying themselves.

Before playing the last game, don't forget to conduct a session of Eco-Ball and make sure that your play area is cleaner than when you began. Show your respect and thanks to the land on which you've played. For a final event, get everyone together in a cooperative group game like Spirals or the Lap Game. And before you leave, make plans with your new friends to play together again.

We've mentioned some of the ways you can help make New Games work, but you'll learn much more about New Games by playing them. Most importantly, stay in touch with the people with whom you're playing. Adapt the games to them. The Player-Referee is not there to monitor the game—she or he is there to serve the players. That's all there is in New Games. There are no standings, no stars, no spectators—just people playing, hard and fair, with nobody hurt. ■

Games for Two Dozen

VERY ACTIVE
Snake-in-the-Grass
Siamese Soccer
Dho-Dho-Dho
Great Plains
Slaughter
British Bulldog
Blob

ACTIVE
Rock/Paper/Scissors
Orbit
New Volleyball
Hug Tag
Caterpillar
Skin the Snake
Bug Tug

MODERATE
Vampire
The Mating Game
Islands
Ooh-Ahh
Pina
Prui
Hagoo

Snake-in-the-Grass

The very first New Games Tournament invited everyone to bring their own new games—and some did. Wriggling on his belly like a snake, a ten-year-old boy showed everyone the game he had brought. It was such a hit that, sure enough, the second New Games Tournament roped off a special area for Snake-in-the-Grass.

The starter snake lies down on the ground on his stomach. Everybody else gathers fearlessly around to touch him. (One finger will suffice—you don't want to get too close to a snake.) When the Referee shouts, "Snake-in-the-Grass!" everybody runs, staying within the bounds of the snake area, while the snake, moving on his belly, tries to tag as many as he can. Those touched become snakes, too.

Non-snakes run bravely around in the snake-infested area, trying to avoid being caught. (For your own sake and the snake's sake, take off your shoes and watch out for snake-fingers.) The atmosphere gets even better if all the snakes are hissing. The last person caught is the starter snake in the next game.

A field full of writhing, hissing serpents can be a scene of horror or wonder, depending upon whether you're a dualist or a herpetologist. Either way, a game that starts with one snake and ends up with all snakes must be a social commentary of some sort. ■

Siamese Soccer

This game didn't originate in Southeast Asia, but Barnum's famous twins did; hence the name for this variation on the world's favorite professional sport. The way we play it is singularly unprofessional.

Set up for a regular game of soccer: teams, goals, boundaries, etc. You might want to make the field a bit smaller, though, and have about 20 players on each side. The only modification on regular soccer rules is that the players on each team have to pair up and tie their ankles together in three-legged race fashion. You can kick the ball with either your free foot or your "big foot." The goalie might be comprised of two people tied back-to-back at the waist. (These supplemental rules are not likely to be adopted for World Cup competition.)

You'll probably spend a lot more energy gallumping around the field with your twin than you will actually chasing the ball. We suspect that even having Pele himself on your Siamese Soccer team couldn't assure you of victory.

If you'd like to add another dash of random craziness, why not use a rubber football from a variety store? Why not have two balls—one for each team—going simultaneously? Three teams? One goal in the center? Try anything! ■

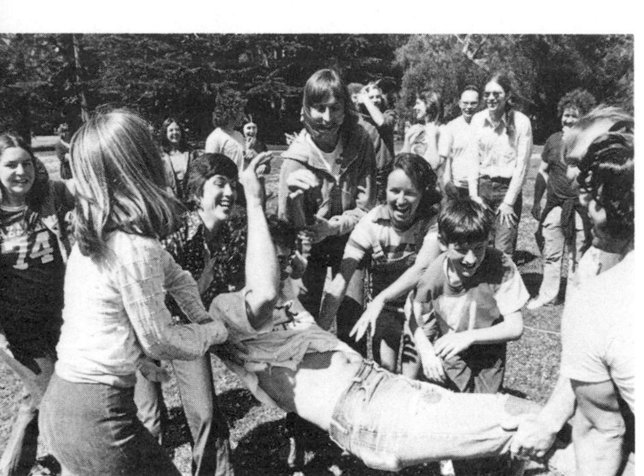

Dho-Dho-Dho

Here's a game in which being the smallest can definitely be an advantage—but so can being the biggest. It all depends on how quick you are and how long you can hold your breath. Because of its emphasis on agility and breath control, this game has also earned the name of Yogi Tag.

Your playing arena should be a surface soft enough to cushion a fall. The beach, your back lawn, or a gym mat are suitable. Divide the area into two equal parts with a center line.

Players, in two teams, stand on either side of this border, leaving a no-man's land between them. One team chooses a player to make a foray across the line, tag one or more players on the other side, and return safely home. Clearly that could require agility—but breath control? That's where the "dho-dho-dho" comes in.

Before crossing the center line, the player who is IT takes a deep breath. Not only must he complete his mission in one breath, but he must use that breath to repeat aloud in a steady, rapid flow, "Dho-dho-dho-dho-dho-dho. . ." If members of the opposite team can catch and hold him in their territory until he runs out of breath, they've acquired a new team member. If he makes it back across the line with any part of his body, even a fingertip, all those he has tagged join his team.

Overly enthusiastic players who execute running tackles on the dho-dho should be reminded that it's permissible to grasp only *above* the waist. Holding the dho-dho down bodily, though, is entirely encouraged. Adding a rule that the dho-dho cannot be touched until he touches somebody first makes the game less frantic and more inviting to people who fear being pounced on from all sides.

After one team has sent its dho-dho on a foray and everyone is realigned and settled down, the other team sends a raider across the line. The teams keep alternating until everyone is on the winning team.

You may want to play the game for points rather than players. Or you could try an elimination version in which those players tagged by a successful dho-dho must leave the game. In this version, anyone tagged by the dho-dho is out of the game, provided the dho-dho makes it back across on one breath. If the dho-dho doesn't make it home again, *he* is eliminated, and those he has tagged remain. Play until one team disappears.

The struggle for breath can be a pretty powerful impetus to get home. If you've caught a dho-dho, hold on tight. However, during his lingering chant, you might compassionately ease his plight by recalling the alternate name of the game and applying a bit more of the gentle strength of the yogi. ■

Great Plains

This game was inspired by the drama of a buffalo hunt on the North American Great Plains. The cast includes a herd of bison complete with bulls, cows, and a baby calf, and a tribe of Native American hunters riding bareback astride spirited horses. You'll need about 20 players to stage a good spectacle.

About a fourth of the players will be the cow buffalos. They should stand in a circle holding hands, with arms outstretched, then drop hands and each take about three or four steps backwards. Each of the cows puts a Frisbee or other marker on the ground at this point and stands on it. An equal number of players, who will be the bulls, each takes the hand of one of the cows. The herd is completed by placing a playground ball in the center of the circle. The ball represents a baby calf buffalo, vulnerable without any parents, which will be the object of the hunt.

The rest of the players form pairs. One player of each pair, representing an Indian hunter, climbs on the back of his partner, his trusty pony. (Don't feel taken advantage of if you end up being the horse—you won't be for long.)

Now the hunt begins. The object is for an Indian, riding his horse, to break through the circle of the buffalo herd and catch the calf (by kicking the ball). He must do this without being tagged by a bull. The bulls have to keep holding hands with the cows, and the cows cannot move off their markers. If an Indian gets tagged, he and his horse have to go outside the circle and *switch positions* before making another foray into the herd. (Be careful that you don't choose a mount that's much heftier than you are.)

This isn't a game for lone hunters. You'll be able to pierce the defenses of the herd only with concerted and strategic attacks by the whole tribe. When a crafty and agile hunter does finally get through to the baby calf, the hunters and bison herd switch roles. Can you imagine assembling this marvelous cast of characters without having the Indians whooping, horses neighing, and cows and bulls mooing loud enough to be heard from the Black Hills to the Rockies? ■

Slaughter

Stewart Brand invented Slaughter so that people could experience violent and aggressive physical activity without endangering their lives, limbs, and neighborly good feelings. (See page 7 for a history of the game.) Even if you're a confirmed pacifist (especially if you are), don't pass up the chance to play at least one game of Slaughter and discover what softwar has to offer.

The arena is a circle about 30 feet in diameter with a clearly defined boundary. Two holes about a foot wide are dug out at opposite sides of the circle. For the sake of your knees (which will see a lot of action), the playing area should be grass or sand. (For the sake of the earth, if you're not on sand, you might want to use baskets, tires, or other suitable containers instead of digging holes.)

You'll also need a ball for each team. Medicine balls are ideal, but basketballs work fine. You can even use two inner tubes—which makes the game far less graceful but a lot more buoyant.

Divide into two teams with about 20 per side. Everyone takes off their shoes, and

one team also takes off their socks, so teams can be identified. (In a co-ed group, some joker will invariably suggest playing "shirts and skins." At this, the other players have the option of using *him* in place of one of the balls.)

The balls are placed in the holes, and each team, on their knees, forms a huddle around their own ball. At the signal, both teams try to move their ball into the other team's hole. As long as you're on your knees and within the boundaries of the circle, anything goes. In the resulting free-for-all, it's perfectly legal to monopolize the other team's ball, to sit in your team's hole, or to *throw your opponents out of the game.*

It's this last tactic that makes Slaughter the paradigm of softwar. If you can push or lure any part of your opponent's body across the boundary line, he or she is out of the game. It's natural to get a little cooperation from other team members on this one—that's sometimes called "ganging up." (Forcing someone out of the game by threatening to remove their pants really works, but is permissible only as a last-ditch defense against needless aggression.) Sometimes everyone gets so caught up in throwing each other out of the circle that they forget about the balls. (George Leonard's winning strategy is to do just that.) You can also play Slaughter without any balls at all. The name for this variation is "Annihilation."

Slaughter usually draws a gallery of spectators. Besides catching bodies and watching out for their own, they might be good referees if you can't tell, in the midst of the fracas, whether someone has just been thrown out of the circle or a ball has been thrown into the goal.

There's no doubt that this is a game of force. (It's not called Slaughter for nothing.) To keep it a New Game, though, you have to bear in mind that "maximum performance" means not using the *most* force, but using the *least* possible force—and never more than your opponent can handle. If you *and* your opponent ever stop enjoying playing, you've lost the game. ■

British Bulldog

Winston Churchill once explained that the British Bulldog's nose slants backwards so that it can breathe without releasing its grip on its adversary. That's one clue to the nature of this game. For those of you who love challenge and excitement, you can find it here. But British Bulldog also has a distinct appeal for the hardy grandmother and the boisterous two-year-old.

To begin, about one-tenth of the players go to the center of the field and the others to the two "end zones." When the people in the middle call out "British Bulldog 1-2-3!" the other players try to run past them to the opposite ends of the field without getting caught.

The catch is that the people in the middle have to lift the runners off the ground and hold them up long enough to shout out the victory cry—"British Bulldog 1-2-3!" Anyone who is thusly hoisted joins the players in the middle as a catcher.

To be catchers takes a bit of cooperative action, some plotting, and a good deal of consideration for your opponent's well-being. (You don't want to drop anyone on his head or *your* foot.) Remember, the runner you catch becomes your teammate.

In certain cases, it may be necessary to gang up on certain players who defy being levitated single-handedly. Use your discretion, of course. Players who are caught join the people in the middle, so the potential "gangers-up" keep increasing. The game ends when there's no one left to catch or everyone has lost their voices.

This game can be adapted to any nationality. Try playing Borneo Boar, Venezuelan Vicuña, or Kenya Hyena. But in choosing the punchline, keep in mind that the jumbuck may have skipped your tuckerbag by the time you've managed to spit out "Australian Kangaroo 1-2-3!" ■

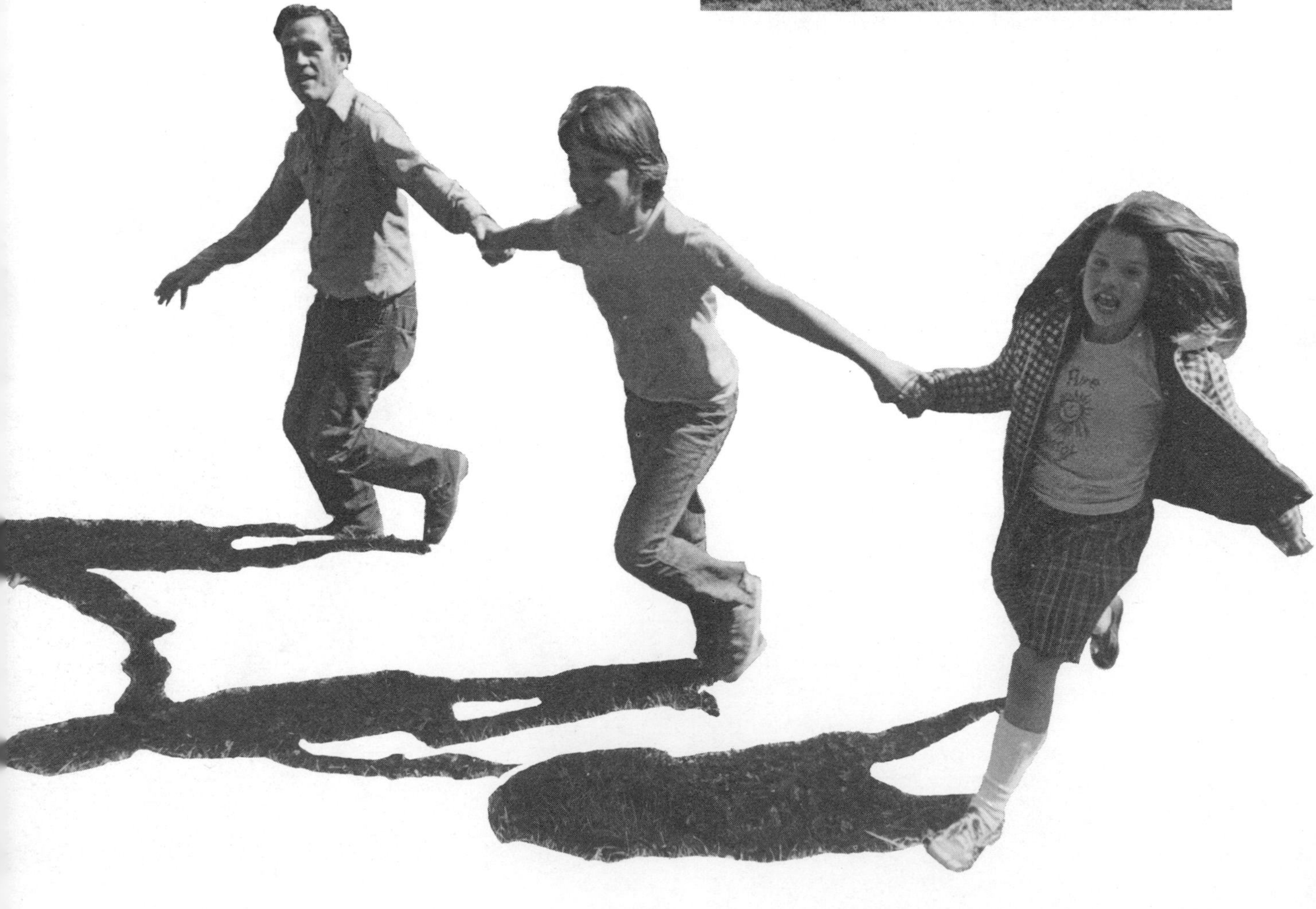

Blob

If you're addicted to late-night TV monster movies, here's a sure way to kick the habit and break out into the light of day. We must warn you, however, that you will not avoid being swallowed up by—the Blob.

The Blob begins innocently enough as a mere individual playing a game of tag. As soon as she catches someone, she joins hands with him. Now he's part of the Blob, too, and they both set out, hand-in-hand, in search of victims. Everyone the Blob catches (only the outside hand on either end of the Blob can snatch at players) joins hands with it and becomes part of the lengthening protoplasmic chain. And thus the insidious Blob keeps growing.

Unlike your run-of-the mill, mad scientist-created Blobs, this one is not content merely to ooze along, seeking its prey. It gallops around the field, cornering stray runners and forcing them to join up. (You'll have to agree on boundaries for this game; some people will go to any lengths to avoid meeting an untimely end at the hands of the primordial slime.)

Moreover (horrors), the Blob can split itself into parts and, with its superior communal intelligence, organize raiding parties on the lone few who have managed to escape. The thrilling climax occurs when there's only one player left to put up a heroic last-ditch stand on behalf of humanity. But alas, there is no defense against the Blob, and humanity succumbs. (If that seems unfair, well, that's the plot.)

The moral of our story could well be, "You become what you fear." If you have the heart to destroy humanity again, you can have the last person caught start the Blob for the next game. ■

Rock/Paper/Scissors

Remember Rock/Paper/Scissors? As kids we played it as a way to choose who went first or who got the extra piece of cake. It was a ritual of fate, complete with chant and symbols. A fist meant Rock, a hand held flat was Paper, and two fingers were for Scissors.

Two by two, we'd face off and chant—one hand beating rhythm in the air—"Rock/Paper/Scissors," and on the next beat we'd throw one of the symbols. The pecking order was: Paper covers Rock, Rock breaks Scissors, and Scissors cuts Paper. One of us came out the winner.

If we weren't playing to get something, we played to *avoid* something—a swift two-fingered swat on the hand or wrist inflicted by the victor. It was a game of chance, but it also took some skill to guess your opponent's move and then cast the conquering symbol. The greatest victory was in being able to "psych him out."

By now, either your nostalgia or your curiosity has been aroused. For this New Games version, we've cut the violence, stepped up the action, and added a bit of group consciousness. What better kind of evolution could you hope for?

You need two teams, a "free zone" for each team, and a center line over which they meet. Each team huddles and collectively decides which symbol they will all throw. (For a group to psych out another group can be pretty interesting.) In two lines, the teams face each other and begin to chant "Rock/Paper/Scissors" and throw their symbols. The team that throws the winning symbol chases the other team, trying to tag as many of their players as possible before they reach their free zone.

It takes a quick eye and lightning response to realize whether you should chase or run. You'll be surprised at how often you get mixed up. (It's a good idea to have a second choice ready in case, at the moment of truth, both teams find they have cast the same symbol. Just begin again with the chant.)

The "old games" way to play would be that anyone tagged is out of the game, until one team eliminates the other. The New Games way is to have all tagged players join the team that caught them. This way teams constantly change numbers and faces, and the game keeps going with everyone in it. (You can test your newly captured teammates' loyalties by seeing whether they'll help you figure out the other side's psychology.)

Although it's said that there's safety in numbers, it seems that there's power in isolation. If you find yourself to be a one-person team, holding your own against twenty-nine people, we'll bet that they'll throw Rock if you throw Paper. ■

Orbit

Seeing the Earth suspended in space can be breathtaking. So is Orbit. In this game, you're the one keeping the Earth up there.

To play, you need two teams and an Earthball. The people on one team lie on their backs in a circle with their heads toward the center and their feet in the air. (No shoes, please!) The other team stands in a circle around them, facing inward.

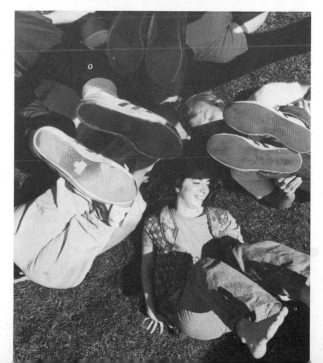

Now toss the Earthball into the center. Those on their backs can touch it only with their feet. Those on their feet can touch it only with their hands. While the Feet are trying to kick the ball into "Orbit" over the heads of the standing team, the Hands are helping gravity a bit by hitting the ball back to the Feet. It's not that the Hands want to keep the Earthball *down*—they simply want to keep themselves *up*, for if the Earthball does soar into outer regions and make a crash landing, the teams switch sides.

Just think, if your team has enough power in its coordinated kick, you might end up launching a new planet. ■

USC

New Volleyball

More than any other standard competitive sport, we've come naturally to play volleyball as a New Game. Although for some people it's as competitive as other traditional sports (if you get a chance, watch the women playing it in the Olympics), for most of us it's basically an easygoing game. The playing is more fun than winning or losing. Based on that principle, here are a few of the New Volleyball games we've tried:

Rotation Ball. A simple way to transform the game and break down team barriers is simply to alter rotation. Play by standard rules, but rotate players (after both sides have served) from one side to the other rather than within each team. This liberates everyone from concern with the score and gets you into just enjoying the game. (Can you imagine playing your heart out in order to win, just to find yourself rotated to the losing side in time for the final point?) It's sort of like playing against yourself—in order to up the score on either side, you've got to give your all. And that's the whole idea.

Volley-Volley Ball. This version of the game changes the scoring system. A team can score from one to three points, depending on the number of times they hit the ball before sending it back across the net. If only one team member hits the ball, only one point is scored. If all three hits are used, the team gets three points. No matter how *macho* your competitive streak is, you'll find yourself popping the ball over to the little kid in the corner or the senior citizen on the side. Ball-hogging just doesn't score. A game is 35 points.

Volley-Volley-Volley Ball. If you've got two teams with a lot of energy *and* a lot of patience, rule that *every* member of the team must hit the ball at least once before it can be sent back across the net. This obviously works best with fewer players and insures them all some action. Play to 9 points.

Infinity Ball. Even more than the other versions, this game is pure cooperation, and any number can play. The rules of standard volleyball still apply, including only three hits per side before sending the ball over the net. The score, kept track of by both teams chanting in unison, is the number of times the ball is hit over the net to the other side without hitting the ground. Any score over 50 is good. Over 100 is phenomenal. And both teams always win.

Creative Ball. Of course, the best variation of all is the one you and your friends make up next time you play. ■

Hug Tag

This variation on classical tag is a perfect example of how you can turn an old game into a new one. Play by whatever rules you're used to, but with one major exception—the only time a player is safe is when he's hugging another player. (No fair for adults to carry small children around under their arms.)

After playing for a while, make the game a little more communal—rule that only three people hugging are safe. Then try four, five. . . everyone. When you're all hugged together, why not get whoever is IT to join you and all have a go at an Amoeba Race? ■

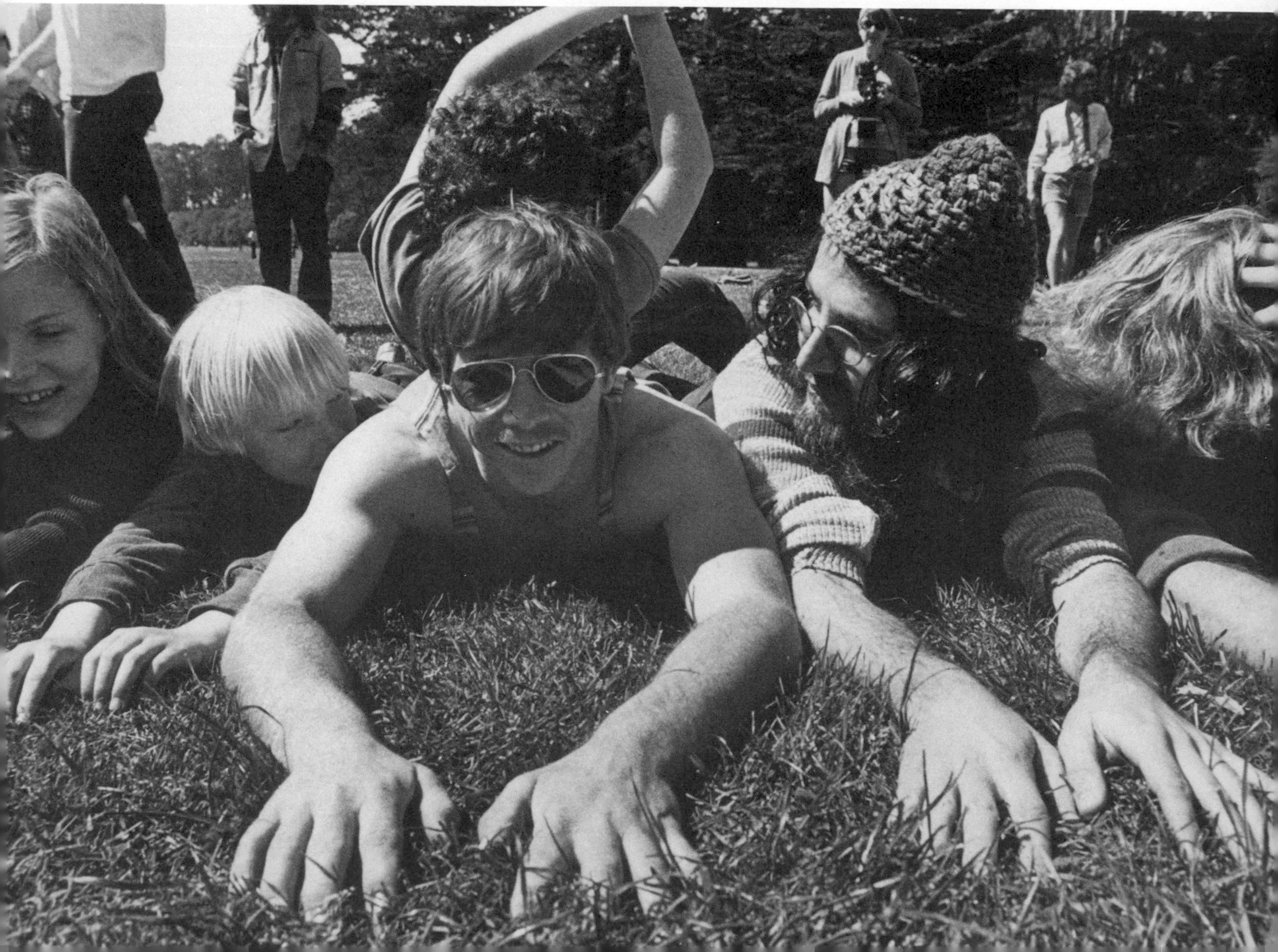

Caterpillar

We used to call this game People Roll, until we grew weary of being asked whether it was a culinary delight for cannibals. By either name, it's a delightful way to knock elbows, knees, heads, and hips with your neighbors.

Get everyone lying on their stomachs, side-by-side. Make sure you're packed really closely together, and have any little people squeeze between two big ones. Now have the person on the end of the line roll over onto her neighbor and keep rolling down the corduroy road of bodies. When she gets to the end of the line, she lies on her stomach, and the next person at the other end starts rolling.

Once you get your momentum going, there'll be no stopping you, as your human caterpillar advances over meadows and hills. How about assembling two caterpillars for a cross-country race? ■

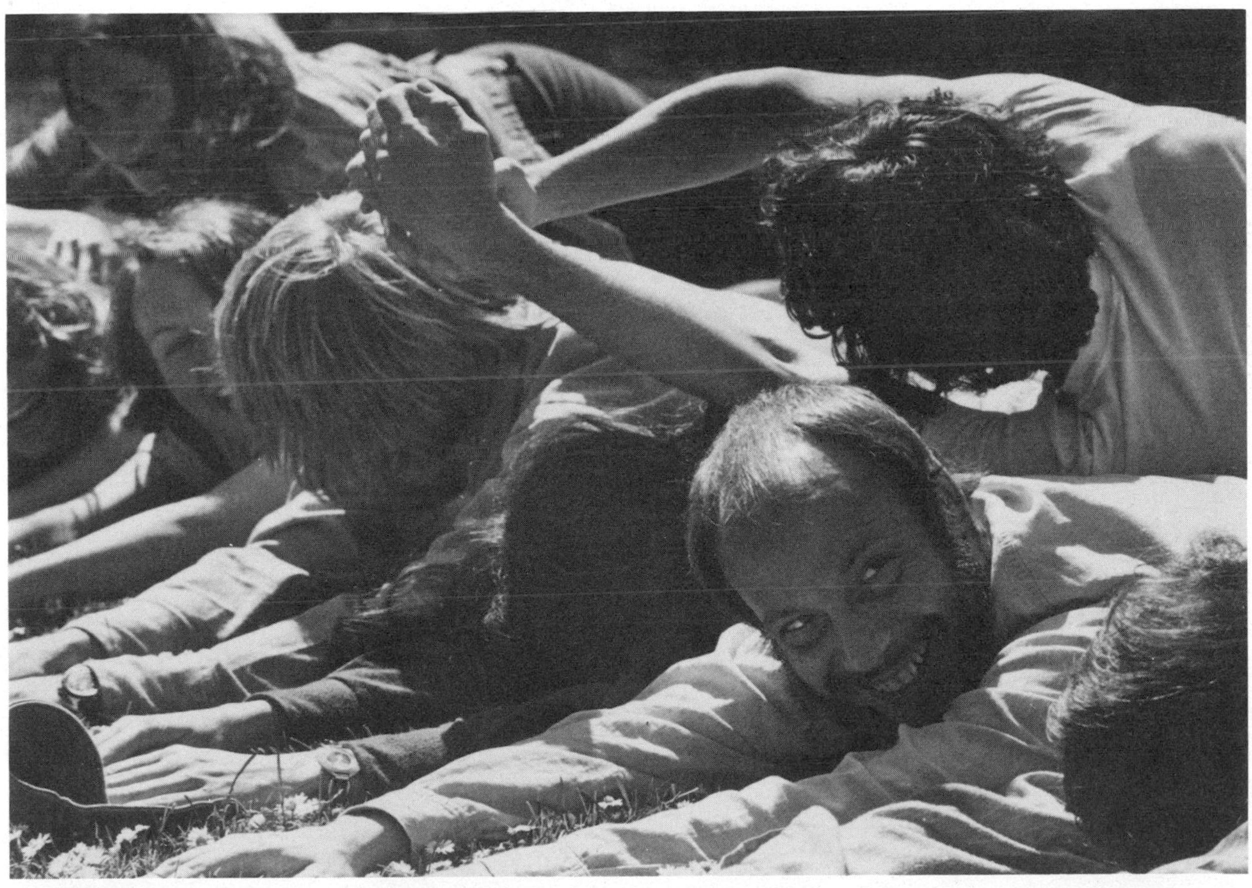

Skin the Snake

This New Games "track-and-field" event places a premium on both individual and group coordination. You can play it as a cooperative exercise, like People Passing, but it's also a great game to play competitively as a race between two teams.

Each team should have about 20 to 25 players, lined up one behind the other. Now reach between your legs with your *left* hand and grab the *right* hand of the person behind you. Meanwhile, the person in front of you is reaching back to grab *your* right hand. (Give it to him, by all means.) Once the chain is formed, you're set to go.

At the starting signal, the last person in line lies down on her back. The person in front of her backs up, straddling her body, and lies down on his back right behind her. (You're all still holding hands, of course.) This continues as the whole team waddles backwards down the growing line of prone bodies and slips into place.

When the last person to lie down has touched his head to the ground, he gets up and starts forward again, pulling everyone else up and along. What just got done gets quickly undone as everyone "Skins the Snake."

When the last person is back on her feet and everyone is in the original chain, still holding hands, get set to run. The winner is the first team that gets *all* its members across the point where the head of the line started. If anyone breaks hands during any part of this process, you must stop, go back to that point, and reconnect before proceeding.

The more you discover about the fine points of the game, the faster you'll get, and vice versa *ad infinitum*—or at least *ad Olympium*. Here are some initial pointers:

You'll be less likely to trip over your teammates if you all take off your shoes. When the line is backing up to lie down, bunch close together so you're all touching. Lie down as close as you can to the person in front of you and put your feet close to his side with toes pointed in. (Some people think it's better to hook your feet around and on top of the person in front. You might check this out with him first.)

When you get down to split-second timing, the players at both ends of the line become all important. The last person to lie down should touch his head to the ground for just an instant, roll back up, and start pulling, being careful not to break the chain. The last person to get up has to be fast and agile and have a really good grip.

Should the lightest players be at the ends or in the middle? We'll leave that for you to experiment with.

We've gone on at greater length here than for most of the games just to illustrate that you can get seriously involved in the strategies, subtleties, and skills of any of our New Games if you and your friends agree to. We could foresee Skin the Snake as a vital event in a future Olympics, as exciting as the crew races and (potentially) as graceful as the gymnastics. Or maybe someday there will be an international spectacle where points are awarded to whomever has the most fun. ■

Bug Tug

Don't have a rope? Try this version of tug of war. You can play it with two—or two hundred.

It's probably easier to try it first with two. Mark a line on the ground or floor. Then you and your partner stand back-to-back on either side of it. Both of you bend forward, reach between your legs, and grasp each other's wrists. Now start tugging and see who gets pulled over the line first.

This particular version of Bug Tug looks great but doesn't last very long. If your partner outweighs you by thirty pounds, you don't stand much of a chance. The best way to get rid of these bugs is to add on a whole bunch more of them.

Stand in two lines, everyone back-to-back. Now one line stands still while the other takes a step to one side. Each of you should now be standing with a person behind you on either side. Everyone bend down and *cross your arms* (this is important) between your legs. Hopefully you'll come across one hand of the person on your right and one hand of the person on your left. Everyone in the line should have a grip on two different people—except the people on the ends. They had best get a grip on themselves.

Once everyone starts pulling, you may get nowhere in particular, but undulating back and forth can be mighty nice. If you get tired of just undulating and feel the urge to get somewhere, how about assembling two 50-person bugs for a centipede race? ■

Vampire

This game comes to us from Transylvania. (Where else?) Although it's not as physically demanding as its next of kin, the Blob, we don't recommend it if you have jumpy nerves or even a mild case of anemia.

To start, everyone closes their eyes (vampires roam only at night) and begins to mill around. You can trust the Referee to keep you from colliding with anything but warm living flesh. However, you can't trust him to protect you from the consequences, for he is going to surreptitiously notify one of you that you are the vampire.

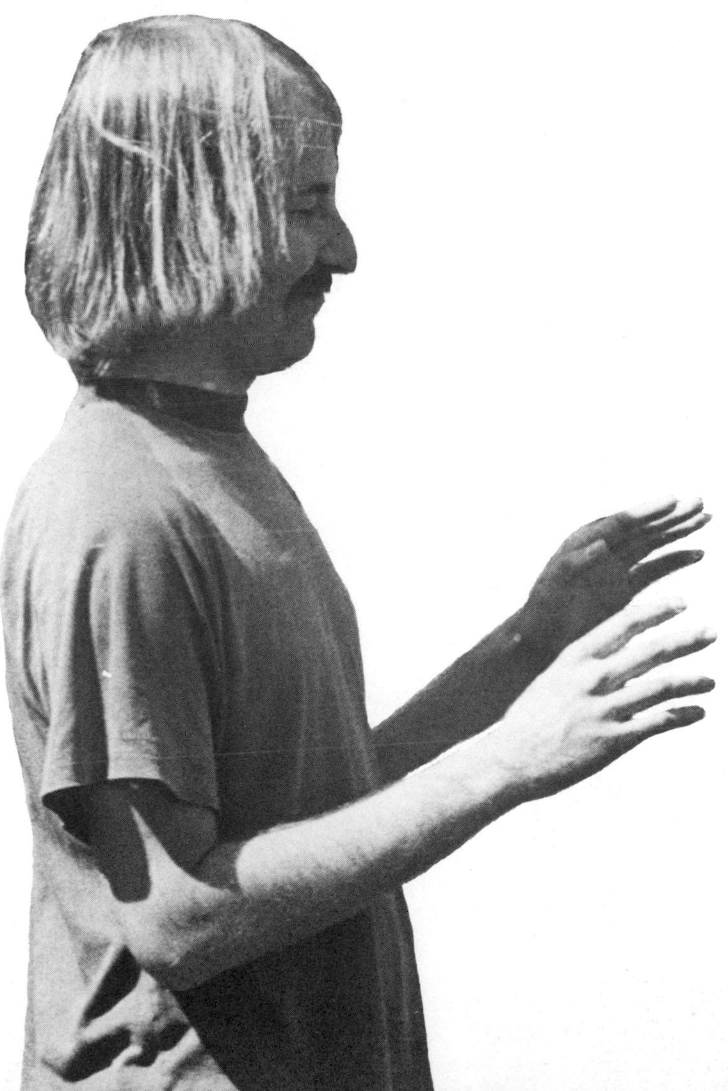

Like everyone else, the vampire keeps her eyes closed, but when she bumps into someone else, there's a difference. She snatches him and lets out a blood-curdling scream. He, no doubt, does the same. (The vampire would be advised to avoid leaving telltale marks on the necks of her victim.) The quality of her performance depends solely upon the authenticity and *élan* with which she executes her snatch and scream.

If you are a victim of the vampire, you become a vampire as well. Once you've regained your composure, you too are on the prowl, seeking new victims. Now perhaps you are thinking that this game too quickly degenerates into an all-monster convention? Ah, but then you didn't know that when two vampires feast on *each other*, they transform themselves back into bread-and-butter mortals.

Will the vampires neutralize each other before all mortals are tainted by the blood-sucking scourge? Why don't you try a little experiment and see. There's always hope, even in the midst of a blood-curdled crowd.

Note: In jurisdictions where Hazardous Toys and Games Legislation has been enacted, we recommend that you place rubber tips on your fangs. ■

GAMES

The Mating Game

Have you ever wondered what Noah and his guests did to pass the time? Or did you ever think of what you might do if you were one of the last Rocky Mountain wolves in existence? Instead of howling at the moon, why not try the Mating Game?

To play your own version, you'll need two sets of cards with names and/or pictures of various creatures. You can use endangered species (to send a little energy their way), mythical beasts, biological oddities—let your imagination roam. The important thing is that there be two of each species—and no peeking at the cards. If you don't have Creature Cards, you may need a Referee who minored in zoology to whisper a beastly name in the ear of each player.

Give everyone a few minutes to tune into their creatures—how they move and talk and feel. Then set them loose to act out their animals by movement and sound. If you find another player making the same beastly antics, then maybe you've found your mate. It will be easier for some to recognize their other half than others. After all, two cats can meow together, but what can two camels do?

When two creatures think they are made for each other, they approach the Referee, expressing their mutual recognition and affection. If the Referee is uncertain as to the advisability of a match, the other creatures can help decide. (However, it might be difficult in these circumstances to discern whether "neigh" means yea or nay.) If the two are officially mated, they can become witnesses to the primal scene or create a supplementary role in the game together. If they don't make it as a pair, they return to the hustle, if not the bustle, of the crowd.

Pandemonium proceeds until everyone is mated. Sometimes a few lone critters get left over. Guided by humanitarian feelings, the Referee and group can engage in a little creative creature-coupling.

The game is best when you choose creatures that are easily identifiable: dragons, chickens, gorillas, anteaters, turtles, whales, bar flies, jail birds, scare crows, parrots, porcupines, paramecia. . . You name it, Noah's got it. ■

Islands

Islands is jokingly called the "Anti-Esalen Game," after the California-based human potential foundation that works to bring people into closer contact. In this game, the object is to *avoid* making contact with anyone.

Place a few Frisbees on the ground, and have everyone start prancing around them, while clapping and chanting or singing. When the Referee signals "Islands," everyone runs to touch a Frisbee. The last person to get to a Frisbee is out. The anti-Esalen feature is that if any two people touch in the process of scrambling for the Frisbees, they're both out of the game. As the group gets smaller, reduce the number of Frisbees until there are only a few people ready to pounce on a single plastic platter.

Another version of this game is simply to see how many people can touch a Frisbee without touching each other. We're not sure what the World's Record for this event is, but we think we can count nineteen people in the photograph on the facing page. ■

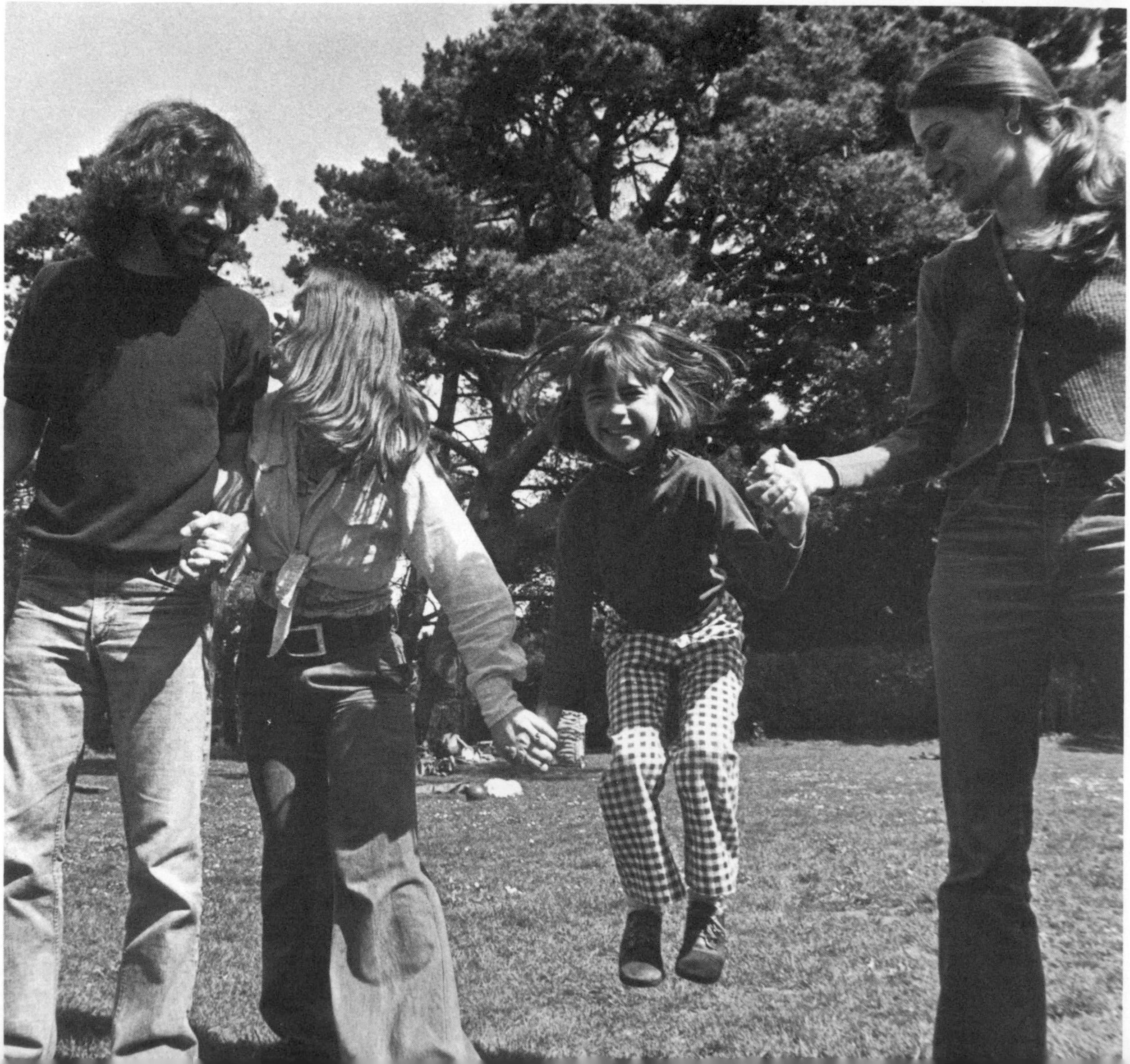

Ooh-Ahh

Ooh-Ahh is as nice a game as it sounds. If you need a break from passing balls, Frisbees, and people, you can try passing handshakes, winks, ooh's, ahh's, and other friendly signs.

Start with everyone standing in a circle holding hands. Now one of you gives a quick squeeze to the hand of the person on your right. This gets passed along to the next person and before you know it, you've got your original squeeze back again, in your left hand.

Keep passing it on until the squeeze is traveling smoothly around the circle. Now speed up the action a bit and add sound. Squeeze and say, "Ooh," and watch it go around. Next add "Ahh," but send it in the opposite direction. Someone is going to get zapped between the Ooh and the Ahh. With a deft exchange, the sounds get sent along their respective ways.

Now try reversing the flow. When someone gives you an Ooh, instead of passing it on, pass it back to them. When both Ooh and Ahh are traveling in the same direction, you can play tag, one trying to catch the other.

After that, you're just about ready for the ultimate: Free-Form Ooh-Ahh. Start a sound, gesture, or combination of them going around the circle. Once it's rolling, transform it: add another action or change a sound. Try tossing it across the circle. You're playing with a pure energy ball! Don't drop it—just keep passing it on. ■

Pina

Take a deep breath and begin reading this game description aloud. If you make it through in one breath, you've got a good start on Pina.

Pina originated with the Nootka Indians of the American Northwest. Stripping alternate branches off a large fern frond, they tried to see how far up the stem they could get in one breath, saying "Pina" for each branch removed.

To prevent unnecessary cruelty to potted ferns and to keep from endangering rare species in park gardens, our version substitutes a circle of people. One person takes a deep breath and begins walking around the circle, tapping everyone on the head and saying "Pina." The idea is to get back to your place before taking another breath. Your success in this game will depend as much on the size of the circle as it does on the size of your lungs.

If you still have some wind left after reading this far, you're in good enough shape to begin practicing for the Big League Breather: Dho-Dho-Dho. ■

Prui

The Prui (pronounced PROO-ee) is a gentle, friendly creature that grows. Bernie DeKoven first told us about it. If you want to get people in touch (literally) and feeling comfortable with each other, introduce them to the Prui.

Unlike the Blob, which everyone avoids, everybody wants to find and become part of the Prui. To do this, everyone stands in a group, closes their eyes, and starts milling about. When you bump into someone, shake his hand and ask, "Prui?" If the other person asks "Prui?" back, then you have *not* found the Prui. Keeping your eyes closed, find another person to ask.

When everybody is bumping about, shaking hands, with strains of "Prui? Prui? Prui?" floating around the crowd, the Referee whispers to one of the players that she is the Prui. Since the Prui can see, she opens her eyes. It seems that the Prui is also a smiling mute, for when someone bumps into her, shakes her hand, and asks that gentle question, she doesn't respond. Ask again, just to make sure: "Prui?" No response. Eureka, you've found the Prui at last!

Now you can open your eyes—you're part of the Prui, too. Keep holding the Prui's hand, and when someone bumps into you, shake with your free hand, and don't respond when he asks. That's how the Prui grows.

You can only shake the Prui's hand at either end, so if you bump into two clasped hands, you know you've got the Prui somewhere in the middle. Feel your way to the end and join it.

Soon enough, everybody's happily holding hands except one or two lost souls groping their way along the line of bodies. When the last stray joins up and opens his eyes, the smiling Prui usually breaks the silence by letting out a spontaneous cheer. ■

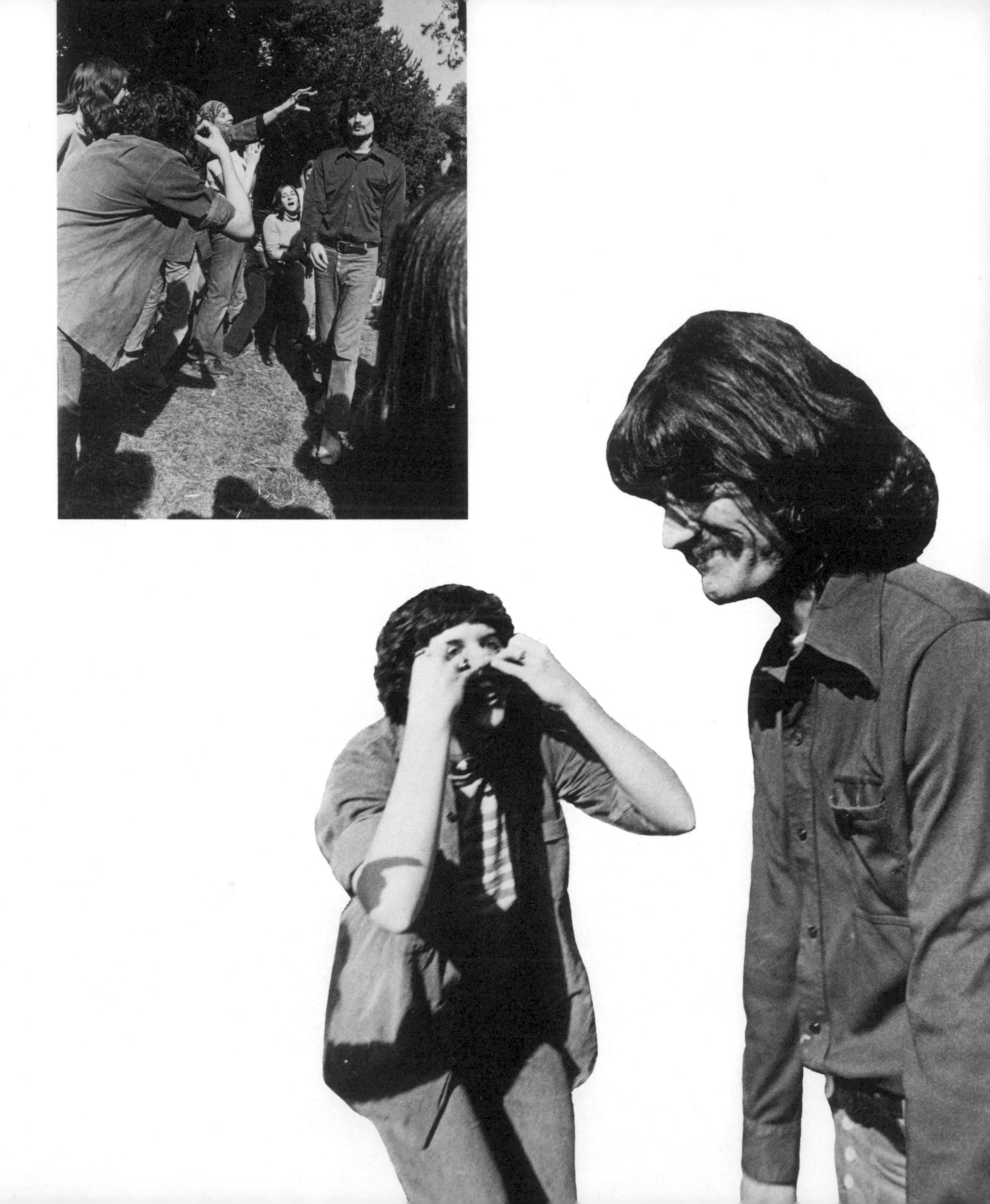

Hagoo

Did you know that it's actually easier to smile than it is to frown? Smiling requires fewer muscles. According to that criterion, Hagoo may be one of our most strenuous games.

In the language of the Tlingit Indians of Alaska, inventors of the original game, *hagoo* means "come here." With that call, they invited a stony-faced challenger to walk a laughing gauntlet without cracking a smile. Our own version of this game looks more like an encounter group doing the Virginia Reel, but since the basic form lends itself easily to changes, you can invent your own dance after you try this one.

To form the gauntlet, two teams stand facing each other in lines about three feet apart. The two players, one from each team, who stand at opposite ends of the lines, are challengers. They step forward and face each other down the length of the gauntlet. With a bow and the invitation "Hagoo," they walk toward each other, breaking neither their eye-contact nor their reserve. In the middle, they pass and continue to the end, determined to suppress their slightest smile or guffaw.

The gauntlet, meanwhile, is alive with the opposite resolve, engaging in any form of facial calisthenics or titillating hullabaloo that might crack the icy determination of the challengers. (A tickle in the ribs, "coo-chicoo" under the chin, or any other form of physical persuasion is off-limits.) There's no telling, of course, which challenger might be prone to which devices, so team members may be torn between a sympathetic and supportive silence for their own candidate and an all-out heckling campaign for the other.

A challenger who successfully runs the gauntlet without revealing the slightest sign of amusement rejoins his own team, free to appreciate his triumph with a smile. But if it's all been too much to take, the challenger doubled up in hysterics gets to contribute his talents to the opposite team by joining up at the end of their line.

The game ends when there's only one team left, or when all players have run the giggling gauntlet, or when everyone decides they're utterly heckled, cackled, and stony-faced out. ■

Theory of Game Change

STEWART BRAND

YOU CAN'T CHANGE A GAME BY WINNING IT, goes the formula, *OR LOSING IT OR REFEREEING IT OR SPECTATING IT. YOU CHANGE A GAME BY LEAVING IT, GOING SOMEWHERE ELSE, AND STARTING A NEW GAME. IF IT WORKS, IT WILL IN TIME ALTER OR REPLACE THE OLD GAME.*

Of course that's only true when you start. Once you restore the children's habit of always messing with your games, then it is the playing of the game that directs the change. A new game begins in a flash, usually, and then grows by degrees.

But grows toward what? Define "better game."

Mostly, I would say, you don't have to worry about this. A "better game" will compel you to play it and refine it. A lousy game will rapidly evaporate for lack of players.

So why bother with theory? All I can answer with is a piece of natural history—the design of one of the most compelling new games of the Twentieth Century, as recalled by its inventor.

The game is Spacewar. It is a game played with computers. It first appeared in 1963, almost instantly proliferated to all computer centers in North America, and still, thirteen years later (a century in the mercurial world of computer design), Spacewar has not been supplanted as the most popular computer game.

It hasn't changed much from its initial design. You have a TV-like screen on which are displayed tiny rockets which are controlled by the players. The rockets can accelerate, turn, and fire torpedoes. When a torpedo and rocket meet, both disappear in an attractive explosion. Often there is a central "sun" on the screen around which everyone orbits (with Keplerian exactness—the closer ones faster). And there are optional additional features such as partial damage, score-keeping, and "hyperspace" (where you can escape in desperation—disappear from the screen for a few seconds and then return at a random location, but with a hazard of perishing in hyperspace that increases each time you use it).

Not long ago I was so impressed with the design of Spacewar that I tracked down its inventor, one Steve Russell. It seems that in 1963 he was just a computer bum in his early twenties employed at MIT's Project MAC (Multiple Access Computer). Here's how he recalls the origin of Spacewar.

> We had this brand new PDP-1. It was the first mini-computer, ridiculously inexpensive for its time. And it was just sitting there. It had a console typewriter that worked right, which was rare, and a paper tape reader, and a cathode ray tube display. Somebody had built some little pattern-generating programs which made interesting patterns like a kaleidoscope. Not a very good demonstration. Here was this display that could do all sorts of good things! So we started talking about it, figuring what would be interesting displays. We decided that we could probably make a two-dimensional maneuvering sort of thing, and decided that naturally the obvious thing to do was spaceships.
>
> By picking a world which people weren't familiar with, we could alter a number of parameters of the world in the interests of making a good game and of making it possible to get it onto a computer. We made a great deal of compromises from some of our original grand plans in order to make it work well.
>
> One of the most important things in Spacewar is the pace. It's relatively fast-paced, and that makes it an interesting game. It seems to be a reasonable compromise between action—pushing buttons—and thought. Thought does help you, and there are some tactical considerations, but just plain fast reflexes also help.
>
> It was quite interesting to fiddle with the parameters, which of course I had to do to get it to be a really good game. By changing the parameters you could change it anywhere from essentially just random, where it was pure luck, to something where skill and experience counted above everything else. The normal choice is somewhere in between those two. With Spacewar an experienced player can beat an amateur for maybe twenty to fifty games and then the amateur begins to win a little.

That I would call damned intelligent use of theory.

Or maybe a better word is "attributes." Russell identified

the attributes of a good computer game and tied them together. "Tie them together" I think means assemble them into a dramatic story, open-ended, starring the player.

When I designed the game Slaughter, which appears in this book, there were certain attributes I was after to jolly and jolt my client, the War Resisters League of San Francisco State College. I wanted something violent but not harmful. (It turned out that bodily pulling is safer than pushing or hitting—hence in Slaughter players are on their knees pulling opponents toward the lethal boundary.)

I wanted a melee quality in Slaughter—everyone simultaneously vulnerable, dangerous, and in combat. I wanted it to be multi-leveled—hence, both the eliminating-opponents and the ball-in-goal features. All these attributes were to serve the grander one of intensity—a game so multiple and fierce that the player is simply lost in it. To up the intensity still further, the game was expressed in life-death metaphor—"any part of your body over the line and you're dead."

That's the creative use of attributes. Let's see what happens when we try analysis, look at existing good games and shake out what they have in common. Here's my list this time. It's suggestive, not comprehensive. I don't know if it could be any use at all in designing games.

Forgiveness. *Volleyball is wonderfully forgiving—any fool can learn the rules and become sufficiently adept almost immediately. People of widely varying skill can play easily together. Teams can be three people or ten. The court can be any old size, the net any height. Compare all those qualities with, say, tennis, which is no fun at all except on a proper court, with enough skill to return the ball (no cinch), and an almost equal opponent.*

Suspense. *In a suspenseful game the issue not only remains in doubt, it increases. The ante goes up. (Indeed, the growing pot in poker is a nice example.) Keeping the issue in doubt may require some of Russell's randomness, so the mighty can fall and have to scramble to recover. Suspense implies climax, which can be drawn out deliciously.*

Keen competition. *I am not one who thinks competition is bad, though I agree over-obsession with losing or winning can be. It is being well-matched that makes a game take off. In a game that pits your everything against a marvelous opponent you can surpass yourself so far that you never quite return. How does this effect game design? Suppose you have evenly matched volleyball teams that are mixed in height and ability. Arrange the rotations so that the tall players always face each other at the net and the short ones ditto.*

Wit. *A game with this attribute is capable of turning inside-out at any point. Hyperspace in Spacewar is a witty feature. The forward pass in football, ever vulnerable to interception, forcing defensemen to run and block and the quarterback to tackle—from expert against expert, suddenly the game is amateur against amateur. There's a certain wit to Hunker-Hawser in this book—you can win by pulling the rope or letting it run, depending on what the other player is doing. It's* *like a joke. The game builds the story. Whoever has the punchline wins.*

Ritual. *For me the only appeal of baseball is its ritual. The business with the bat deciding which team bats first, the stylized infield chatter, the measured slow pace and sudden action. A game that lasts has got to have ritual, the interaction of repetition and surprise, an irrational mythic depth.*

*There's a book you should read—*Homo Ludens*— a study of the play element in culture by Johan Huizinga ($2.95 from Beacon Press). Here's a sample.*

> *Play begins, and then at a certain moment it is "over." It plays itself to an end. . . More striking even than the limitation as to time is the limitation as to space. All play moves and has its being within a playground marked off beforehand either materially or ideally, deliberately or as a matter of course. Just as there is no formal difference between play and ritual, so the "consecrated spot" cannot be formally distinguished from the play-ground. The arena, the card-table, the magic circle, the temple, the stage, the screen, the tennis court, the court of justice, etc., are all in form and function play-grounds, i.e., forbidden spots, isolated, hedged round, hallowed, within which special rules obtain. All are temporary worlds within the ordinary world, dedicated to the performance of an act apart.*
>
> *Inside the play-ground an absolute and peculiar order reigns. Here we come across another, very positive feature of play: it creates order, is order. Into an imperfect world and into the confusion of life it brings a temporary, a limited perfection. Play demands order absolute and supreme. The least deviation from it "spoils the game," robs it of its character and makes it worthless. The profound affinity between play and order is perhaps the reason why play, as we noted in passing, seems to lie to such a large extent in the field of aesthetics. Play has a tendency to be beautiful.* ■

Stewart Brand, creator of the *Whole Earth Catalog* and *Whole Earth Epilog*, conceived of and organized the First New Games Tournament in 1973. He now edits a magazine-format "journal of conceptual news," *The CoEvolution Quarterly* ($8.00 per year from P.O. Box 428, Sausalito, California 94965). This article first appeared in the Summer 1976 issue.

The More the Better

Earthball

The Earthball is the Pied Piper of New Games. This six-foot rubber and canvas globe, painted with continents and oceans, attracts people like the force of gravity. Everyone welcomes the chance to play with the planet, whether they're pushing, passing, or throwing it; kicking or hugging it; on top, beneath, or against it. Some simply gaze in wonder—until the rolling sphere comes bearing down on them and there's nothing to do but bear back.

Earthball games range from the most cooperative to the most competitive in the New Games repertoire. While Chute Ball (page 165) can be a beautiful exercise in group harmony, an all-out game of Tournament Earthball (next page) might reveal the very core and essence of world conflict.

Between these two poles lie endless possibilities for play. Get together with several hundred of your neighbors and let your imaginations and spirits soar. The only rule to remember is: "Play Hard, Play Fair, Nobody Hurt."

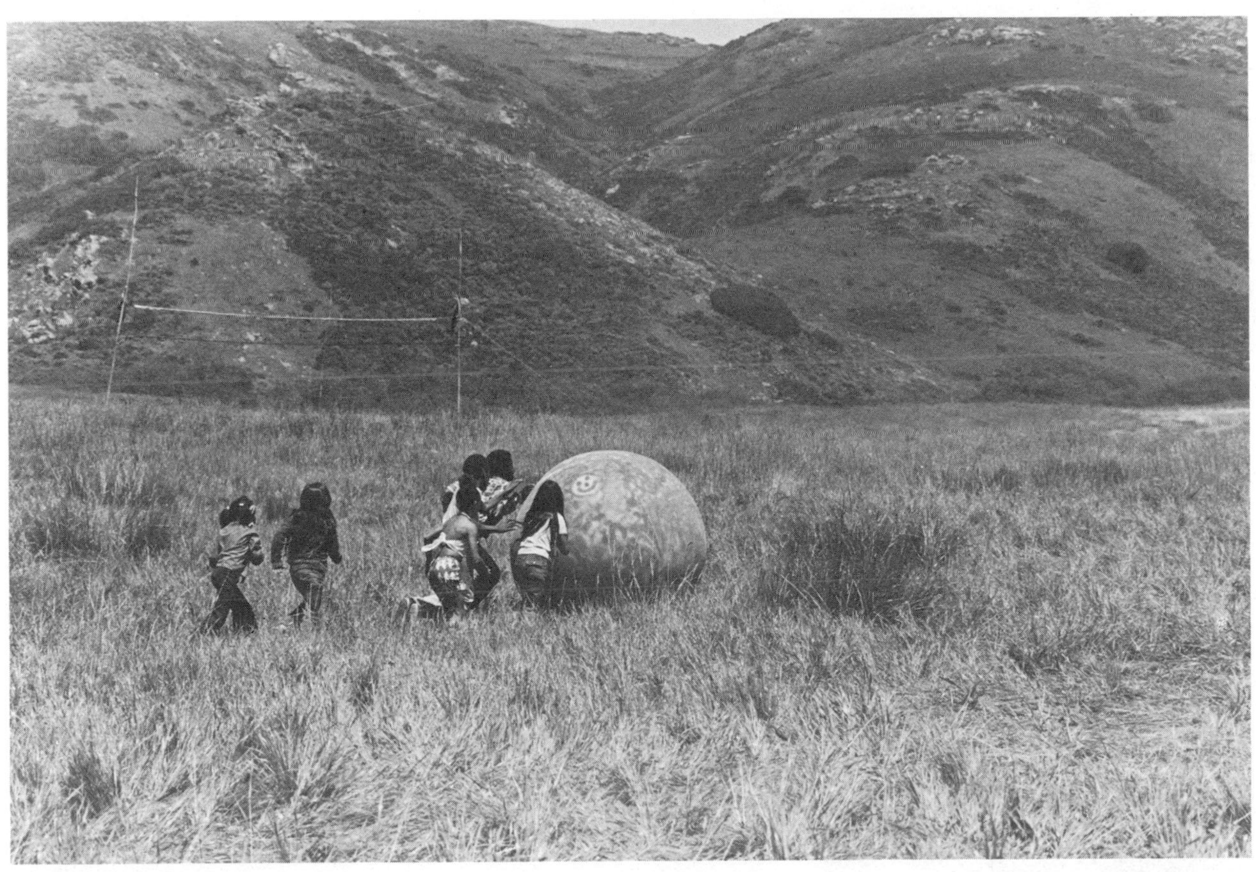

Tournament Earthball. Tournament Earthball is the crowning glory of any New Games event. From the first puff of air to inflate the ball to the final gasp of a retiring competitor, this game is sure to require all you've got. The non-stop forays, clashes, and charges will surely create an atmosphere of pomp and grandeur worthy of trumpets and banners (optional). And it's one game in which the teams are far more likely to change sides than they are to change the score.

The game really begins with the look of disbelief on the gas station attendant's face when that lump of canvas you are inflating starts shaping up like a model of the planet. As the Earth grows, so will the line of people waiting to buy gas, and you'll be obliged to explain the entire game to them. They undoubtedly will be your first successful recruits.

If fitting several thousand cubic inches of air into your car presents a problem, you can roll the ball to your tournament site. This game is called Snowball, and by the time you reach the field, there will be a lot more of you than when you started. If you're nowhere near a gas station and you have a day to spare, you could play Human Airpump as a warm-up before the tournament. (Non-smokers only.)

When you're set to start, all available players are divided into two fairly equal teams. Any fewer than one per team is a bad number. A good number is a hundred or more. An ideal number of players is as many as you have.

Before further action, it's wise for everyone to remove their shoes. (The resulting mass

of footgear can be lined up as boundaries.) The teams move to either extremity of the field and the Earthball is rolled into place in the center of the arena.

Referees should make sure that all players are behind their respective goal lines. (Any team that fails to attempt a bit of creative cheating should be eliminated as hopelessly dull.) If teams have specific names, such as "Red" and "Blue" or "Here" and "Now," members can chant the team name to build spirit and intimidate the opposition.

When the line-ups look relatively stable, and the troops are sufficiently fired up, the Referee asks, "Are you ready?" (A bullhorn is an obvious asset.) If the answer comes like rolling thunder and the ground begins to shake, the Referee should withdraw to a safe position and, in his most convincing Seventh Cavalry bellow, let loose with: "Charge!"

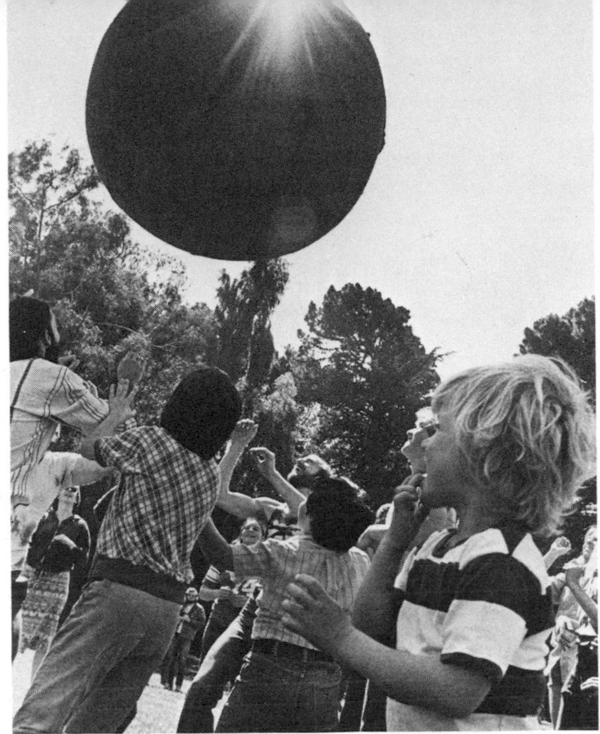

So begins the epic struggle to push, lift, throw, blow or by any means advance the ball past the opposing team's goal. Initially, the ball may not advance at all. People pile up on both sides of it, and they may as well be pushing stone as rubber. If enough pressure is applied from either side, the only way out for the ball is up. When it does finally lift off, major movements begin. At this point, the referee should urgently remind everyone of the "Play Fair" and "Nobody Hurt" parts of the New Games credo. (In this game, people seem to "Play Hard" naturally.)

Once the ball gets moving, it rolls fast and firm. If you and it are rolling in opposite directions, something's got to give—and it won't be the ball. You can either leap out of the way, do a lightning about-face and move faster in the same direction, or suffer the more common fate of being somewhat flattened in its path.

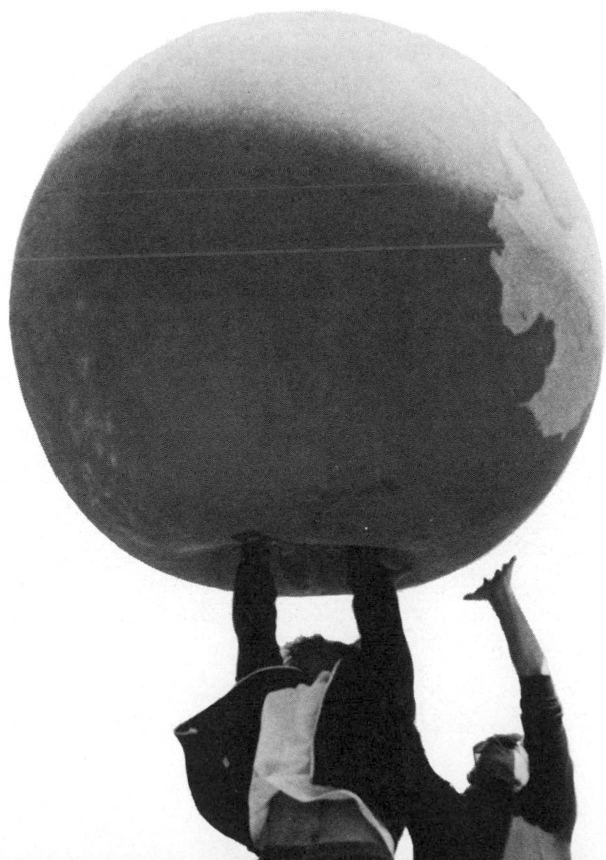

The only way to stop a ball headed for a goal is to recruit a mass large enough to alter its course. No problem. If enough spectators don't join the underdog side, players from the other team usually will. (Earthball games seem plagued with a high incidence of turncoats and defectors.)

Should a goal occur within the first several days of play, a temporary halt to action is called. The ball is returned to center field and all players gather around. The Referee then announces: "The score stands at One to Zero—we'll play to 21, win by 2." At this point, the Referee should retreat, hastily.

Humane Earthball. These variations on the basic game were invented by a group of "walking wounded" from one of the early Tournament Earthball matches. The resulting games retain most of the delightful craziness of their predecessor, but don't require as much personal wisdom and restraint on the part of the players, so everyone is more likely to "Play Fair."

In the "Crab Variation" everyone has to travel on their hands and feet with their backs toward the ground and can only kick the Earthball with one foot. To keep the game clean, we suggest that everyone first remove their shoes.

Add a rule that everyone must remain on their knees. This will slow down the game considerably and greatly reduce the chances of your being overtaken by hordes of your opponents on the rampage. Unless you are willing to make an old pair of pants into your permanent official Earthball uniform, you'll need to discover a good remedy for removing grass stains from your knees. For that reason, we've called this game the "Clorox Variation."

In the "Bump," the only permissible point of contact with the ball is your rear end. Just make sure that while you're all bending down to make contact with the ball you don't inadvertantly make your skulls into targets. Bumping heads can be a good way of getting to know your opponent, but not necessarily the most pleasant. Humane Earthball is your chance to discover which ways are. ■

Clench a Wench

O.K., we truly apologize to everyone—male and female—who's trying to improve the quality of their feminist consciousness. But it's such a terrific rhyme and obviously results from a language limitation. So by unanimous vote of the New Games Foundation (3 women and 3 men), the name of this game remains "Clench a Wench."

Enough of semantics, and on with the game. It's nothing less than a madcap relay race, with men carrying their female partners around the course. (In case you're wondering, that exemplary couple in the photo are All-Star Referee Ron Aarts trucking New Games Guiding Light Pat Farrington in the memorable Clench a Wench relay of the First New Games Tournament.)

If you women feel discriminated against and deprived of the chance to show off your own stamina, how about carrying the men. "Clench a Mensch"? ■

Tug of War

This is probably the oldest New Game. And absolutely everyone can play—including the neighborhood mongrel champing at the frayed end.

Just get a long fat rope, divide into two teams, and pull like crazy. When your side begins losing ground, rally passers-by to your rescue. Who could resist joining a nearly defeated tug team, knowing that her efforts might turn the tide? Why, it's even been known for players from one team to joyfully become turncoats, just to prolong the tug. It's the old "the-more-you-give-the-more-you-get" principle.

For a variation on the traditional game, we've adapted a technique from the famous auto races at LeMans: Have everyone wait ten feet back from the rope and, at the signal, scramble for position. Or try it with the rope stretched across a creek or mud hole, or through a sprinkler. The real winners in this version are the children on the losing team who get a free ride through water or (oh boy!) mud.

How about a game of Tri-Tug, with three teams, a three-ended rope, and three markers (Frisbees do the job)? Put one marker on the ground beneath each rope, about ten feet back from the center knot. Now each team tries to pull the center over its own marker. There are some subtle strategies involved in a threesome. Why not discover what they are? ■

Earth Volley

Volley with an Earthball, anyone? It's basically the same game as volleyball—except for the few minor adjustments called for by playing with a ball 200 times larger than usual. For instance, in the standard version, only three people on a side are permitted to touch the ball before passing it over the net. It takes at least that many just to support an Earthball, let alone loft it up and over. We're confident that once you start playing, you'll devise your own ingenious strategies. The game ends when the net concedes. ■

People Pass

John O'Connell reports that the first People Passing spectacle he ever witnessed was in the University of Michigan football stadium. When all of the stadium's 150 rows were filled with people who were getting a bit bored with the game, some creative chaps would grab someone from row 1 and start passing him over their heads—destination, row 150. Everyone seemed to have a lot of fun with this, but if you were the "passee," there was always that nagging fear that a touchdown would be scored just as you reached row 149. Oops, over the wall!

In our version, we've eliminated the football game, so everyone can be sure of a smooth ride and a gentle landing. Have everyone stand facing forward in a double line, and make sure that the passers are standing as close together as possible. (Many hands make light work.) One person at the head of the line leans back, and is hoisted up to start her high, hand-delivered journey over the multitudes. When was the last time you received such a lift? ■

Amoeba Race

Here's your chance to experience consciousness at the cellular level. To begin, you'll need a lot of protoplasm, a cell wall, and a nucleus. Protoplasmic people should be those who don't mind being close. Those who like to contain themselves (and others) would make a good cell wall. They should surround the protoplasm, facing outward, and link elbows. Someone with good eyesight and the ability to keep on top of things should be the nucleus, seated on some shoulders of the protoplasm. Now you are an amoeba!

Try a trip down the field or around the block. A rhythmic chant might be helpful for coordinating movements. (What sort of sound does a one-celled creature make?) Now try a little cell division. Pull yourself in two, hoist up a second nucleus, and see which amoeba gets to the other end of the field first. Whether you make it or not, you're sure to develop some real appreciation for single-mindedness. ■

BEACH
DELAWARE

Parachute Games

We're told that Leonardo Da Vinci invented the parachute, but never tried it out because he couldn't figure out a way of getting airborne. If he'd only kept his thoughts and feet on the ground, he could have at least played a few New Games. Get hold of a used parachute from a surplus store and about 25 to 50 people from the neighborhood to hold on around the edge and you're set for an afternoon of merriment.

First you'll probably just want to play at flapping the chute together—letting it billow up, loft for a moment, and then drift down on a cushion of air. See how well you can work together to bring the chute to its full expanse. Now lift the chute and all run to the center, as you create a giant mushroom that envelopes you in its folds. Run to the outside again. This time, pull the chute up and over you, and sit down on it. When you're all seated in a circle in a nylon cocoon, rock back and forth in your own private world.

Take up your positions around the edge of the chute again, and count off by three's so you're divided into three evenly interspersed groups around the rim. Now get the chute rising and falling again, and at the signal have all the "Number Ones" run underneath and exchange places with another of their number on the other side. See if you can all make the switch without letting the chute touch you, but watch out for mid-chute collisions. Try again with the Number Twos and Threes. For a mad-cap finale, have everyone run under and try to find a new space before the chute catches them.

Stand around the rim and flap the chute randomly so it makes ripples. Call out letters of the alphabet and march around on mountains of air when your first-name initial is called. If you're getting overheated from all this flapping, running, and prancing, take turns lying under the chute while everyone else creates a mammoth people-powered air conditioner for you.

Toss some playground balls into the center of the chute and practice popping them into the air, or choose sides (we'll leave the number and arrangement to your imagination) and see who can shake the balls over the heads of the other team(s). And if by chance you're fortunate enough to have both a parachute *and* an Earthball, well, just turn the page for the granddaddy parachute game of them all.

Thank you, Leonardo. ■

Chute Ball

Usually parachutes float back to Earth. In this game, you can turn things around and get the Earth floating back to the parachute.

Have everyone hold a parachute around the edge, like a fireman's net, and toss in an Earthball. With a little coordinated effort, you'll send it soaring. With a little more, you'll catch it on the descent and send it off again.

If you like competition, divide into two teams and have one side try to roll the ball off the chute and over the heads of the other team.

For the ultimate in group coordination, get the Earthball rolling around the edge of the parachute. To keep it moving on the chute without its flying off requires a steady wave-like motion, with the Earthball nestled just ahead of the crest. The rhythm, harmony, and cooperation this entails makes the game as beautiful as it is challenging. ■

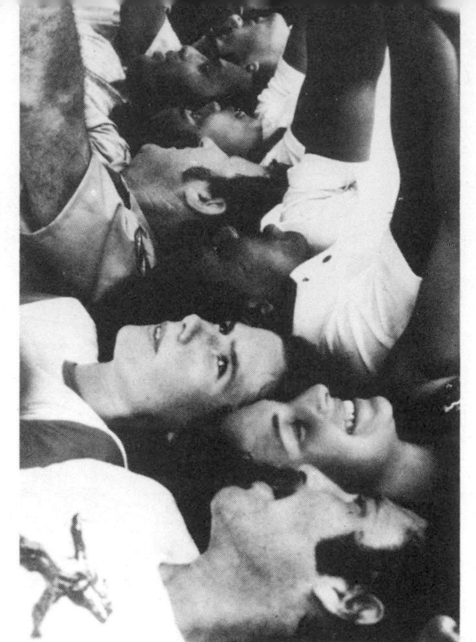

Planet Pass

Unlike Orbit, in which you have to launch your own planet, this gentle game requires only that you keep it on course.

To play, everyone form two lines and lie down on your backs with your heads toward the center. Raise your hands and start passing the Earthball down the line. (If the Earth starts to get away from you, you can give it a little tap with your foot.) To keep the Earth moving along, run to the end of the line as soon as you've passed the ball and lie down to receive it once again.

Since this game could obviously continue *ad infinitum*, maybe you should devise a scoring system for the players—and the Earthball—to accumulate points. Or if you're taken with the potential for metaphysical imagery, why not set up two goals, one in time and one in space? After 2001 goals, the game starts over. ■

NEW GAMES
Play Hard
Play Fair
PARRIS
24

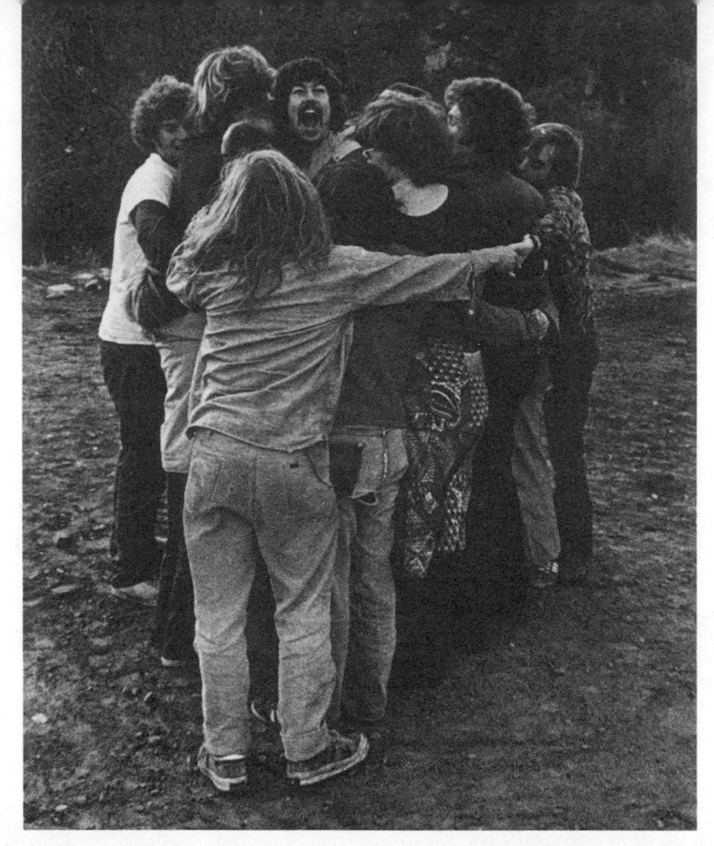

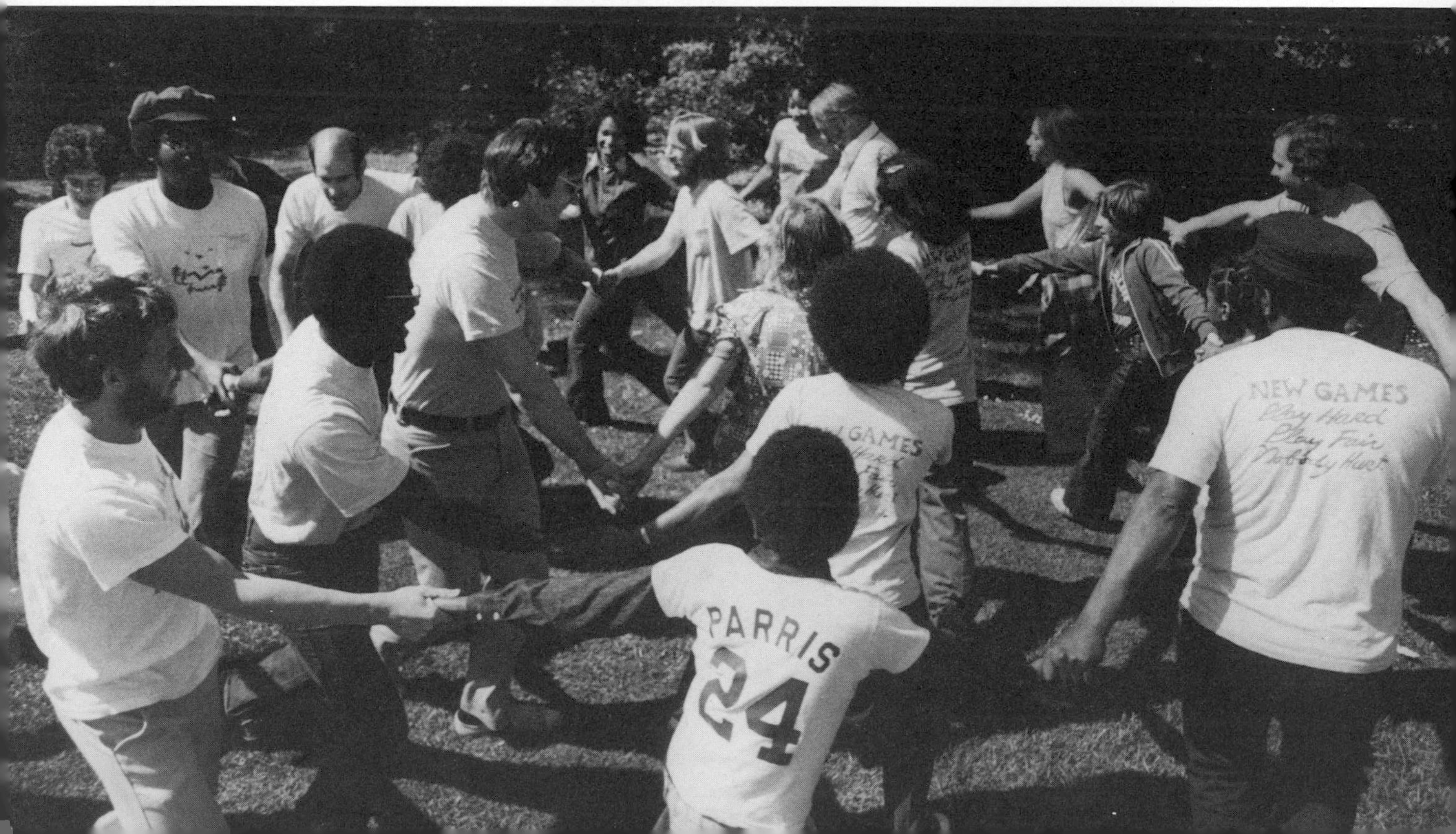

Spirals

After a 100-point game of Infinity Volleyball or a devastating round of Slaughter, the group energy may be a little ragged and dispersed. Making Spirals is a fine way to gather it back together again, let everyone catch their breath, and get the group to give itself a big hug.

To begin, everyone joins hands in a circle and pauses for a few minutes to feel the group coming back together. Then one person releases the hand of her neighbor and, pulling the giant human rope behind, begins to walk around the outside of the circle. The other person who broke hands remains in position.

The chain of people spirals 'round and round the stationary person, drawing everyone into a tighter and tighter coil until all the players—still holding hands—are wrapped around each other, closer than the stars in Andromeda Galaxy.

Now feel the group energy. You're all one body. You might decide to sway together or to express how you are feeling in sound.

The best way to unfold the spiral is from the center. Still holding hands, the person in the middle ducks down (everyone will have to make a little room for her) and begins to crawl out through the forest of legs. The whole group follows down and through, magically uncoiling. When you're all unwound, you should be in a circle again—and much more one being than when you started.

Note: If you plan to play this game in Argentina, remember that spirals in the Southern Hemisphere tend to turn inward in a clockwise direction, while Northern Hemisphere spirals prefer to go counterclockwise. ■

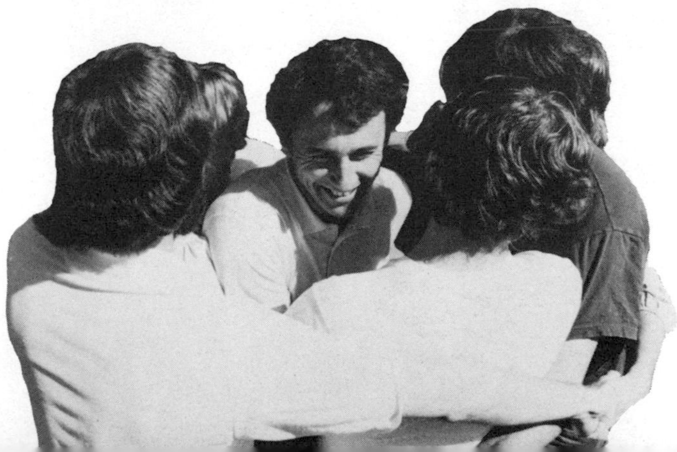

The Lap Game

After a strenuous stretch of whopping, boffing, clenching, and tugging, how about sitting down for a rest—New Games style?

Everyone available stand in a circle, shoulder-to-shoulder. Now turn to the right. Then, *very gently*, everybody sit down on the lap of the person behind them.

There are two ways you can get yourselves into this position. The "Slow and Easy" method is to have one person lie on his back with his knees bent. The next person sits down, forming a nice chair for the next person to sit on, and on and on until the whole circle is seated. The crucial moment comes when the person on his back is hoisted up onto the lap of the person behind him. And there you have it—a sitting circle.

The "Fast and Reckless" method is for everyone to sit on their neighbor's lap at precisely the same moment. This is very impressive when it works and a spectacular flop when it doesn't. Actually the circle is far more stable, if less exciting, when you sit on your neighbor's *knees*. (Somehow, "The Knee Game" just doesn't have the same ring to it.)

Once you're comfortably seated, you might all wave your arms, or give the person in front of you a back rub, or even *try* a caterpillar merry-go-round. Next to tickling, that last suggestion is the surest way to end the game.

We're told this game was originally called "Empress Eugenie's Circle," after the Austrian Empress's account of how her soldiers kept dry while resting in a wet field. It's just too bad they didn't try playing it with the Prussians.

The Lap Game World's Record. Since there's no limit to the number of people that can play the Lap Game, a World's Record attempt was probably inevitable.

The first claim to championship came from 309 people in Davis, California, on November 9, 1974. This was followed by 710 who sat together at the "Great Earth Festival" in Costa Mesa, California, on October 19, 1975. The City of Costa Mesa wrote to *The Guinness Book of World Records* to establish their claim. However, by the time Guinness had received their letter, the *Irvine* (California) *World News* for October 31, 1975, had reported the successful seating of 1,048 people. (The Costa Mesa folks challenged the Irvine record on the grounds that the participants didn't sit on each other's knees; some were half-standing—shocking!)

Meanwhile, unbeknownst to any of the contenders, the World's Record had apparently already been set on May 6, 1974, by a humble group of 1,306 in Auckland, New Zealand (proving that neither the world nor the lap-sitting mania is confined to California). This record has since been superceded by 1,468 dedicated students in Palos Verdes (in guess what state) as reported in the *Los Angeles Times* for November 9, 1975. And the beat goes on.

If you plan to try for the World's Record, just make sure you have fun doing it. As far as we're concerned, though, we haven't really set the record straight until we've got every inhabitant of the planet comfortably snuggled in the lap of his or her neighbor.

Here's a World's Record everyone can try for. How *few* people can sit on each other's laps? ■

Eco-Ball

Eco-Ball is the culmination of New Games. As such, it has traditionally been held as the *Grand Finale* at New Games tournaments. Everybody plays. A little music fits the occasion just fine—your own jug band, some of the local high school marching band—or, in lieu of live musicians, background music from the Keystone Cops sets a good pace. This is the one and only game in which accumulated points count toward the Official New Games World Championship Series. Curious? Here's how to play:

Participants split up into as many teams as you want or feel are necessary. The entire tournament site (including play, rest, food, and sanitation areas) is divided into a like number of parts. The boundaries should be clearly described but not marked. Each team is given one portion of the field. Basic equipment for the game includes plastic garbage bags and nimble fingers.

The teams all huddle and, at the starting signal, they're off, setting out to pick up whatever's lying around and littering their areas. (You can't be shy of ooky fingers in this game.) If you're unsure whether a particular bit of litter is in your area or not, go ahead and pick it up. Anything that doesn't fit with the natural environment is fair game. (Billboards, parking lots, and fast food franchises should be left intact, unless you're playing by the optional "Conservation Guerilla" rules.)

When the Referee sees that the teams have exhausted all possibilities for play and/or themselves, the end of the playing period should be called. The teams regroup and empty the contents of their bags into the goal. (The goal should be ample enough to hold everything securely, and transportable enough to get it all to a disposal site.) Music, cheers, and applause favorably accompany each goal scored.

According to the standard scoring system, one point is awarded for each bit of litter that can be identified as having originated with the New Games tournament, and two points for each bit that was on the playing field prior to the tournament. The Referee should resolve scoring disputes, but she might summon the opinions of the participants. The team with the most points is declared the Eco-Ball Local Champion.

International Competition. If you would like to enter your group in the New Games Eco-Ball Championship Series, total the points from all teams and send us the final score, along with a brief description of the playing field and number of participants. (Please send no boxtops, poptops, chewing gum wrappers, or banana peels.)

Eco-Ball can be played anytime—not just at the end of New Games tournaments. Why not have a game in your neighborhood this weekend? ■

Recipe for a New Games Tournament

A New Games tournament doesn't have to be planned, publicized, and organized on a grand scale. One of the most delightful ways to play New Games is spontaneously. Simply get together with your co-workers, classmates, or family in your local park, recreation center, or a meadow. You don't need any special equipment—just bring along a few of your favorite New Games ideas, a picnic lunch, and the desire to play. If people gather to watch, invite them to join. Let your only goal be having fun together. By day's end, you will have staged as successful a New Games tournament with twenty-five of your friends and neighbors as you could have with twenty-five hundred.

A New Games tournament can also be a way of bringing the people of a whole community together—to celebrate a holiday, to open a park or community center, to share ethnic and cultural backgrounds, or, like our annual tournaments in San Francisco, to create an opportunity for businessmen and babies, grandpas and musicians to meet each other as members of a play community. Preparing for a large tournament is also a way for people of the same city or village to discover each other and share their abilities and resources in creating an event that everyone can enjoy.

What follows are some of the guidelines and pointers we have learned during the course of preparing for our large-scale tournaments. They can serve as a checklist and starting point for your own preparations. Allow yourself plenty of time to take care of all the details, and remember that it is not the game you play that counts, but how you play it.

People. *The individuals and groups contributing to your tournament can reflect the ability of New Games to include everyone. Involve senior citizens, scouts, singles' clubs, theater groups, growth groups, schools and colleges, churches, businesses, community centers and youth clubs, civic park and recreation leaders, political organizations, playschools, and the media. Skilled people who will volunteer their services are often found in the fields of recreation and education, but don't limit yourself to directly related institutions. Often large corporations, for example, have employee recreation programs that would be interested in taking on a project.*

To create a tournament requires many volunteers willing to perform a whole range of services, from office work and designing and distributing posters to staffing the information center at the tournament and collecting garbage. In some cases, volunteers can perform a dual function, e.g., performing artists can do their act while coordinating traffic or refereeing games. People are the major resource of a New Games tournament. As an organizer, if you remember that everyone is co-creating the event, you'll remain open and flexible to all expressions and contributions.

Site. *Depending on the weather, the nature of the event, the number of people you expect, and the facilities available to you, tournament sites can range from gymnasiums, school auditoriums, or store fronts to vacant lots, neighborhood parks, farms, or the broad valleys of a state recreation area. You'll need approximately one acre of space for every 500 people at the event. One of the interests of New Games is to increase the use of public lands and parks by the citizens who own them and to encourage a harmonious relationship between the land and the people using it. Be sure to stress this environmental policy when applying for permission to use a certain site. Since the classic New Games tournament is staged in an open field, the following remarks will relate mainly to events held outdoors.*

The site you choose should be easily accessible to all participants. If players plan to reach the site by car, adequate parking space should be available and arrangements made for coordinating traffic flow. To eliminate the pollution and congestion that can be caused by a mass convergence of automobiles, encourage carpools. You might consider setting up a switchboard before the event to get riders and drivers from the same area in touch with each other. Be sure to notify the police and highway patrol so that they can help with traffic supervision.

If you are not arranging special transportation as we did for our Second New Games

Tournament, then select an area near public bus routes. Invite your city transport lines to participate in the event by supplying extra vehicles for the day. (A New Games event can be an incentive for your community to experiment with mass transit systems.) All transportation arrangements should take into account not only the needs of the people but the impact on the land and atmosphere of the event as well.

Every attempt should be made to keep the playing area natural.

Unless you are celebrating the opening of a new park area, keep in mind that people may be reluctant to venture out to an unfamiliar site. In any case, it is wise to include in your publicity a good map that indicates how to get to the site from major public points and information on appropriate public bus routes.

Once you have procured a site and completed arrangements for its use with the land owner or governmental agency in charge, get to know the area. A group clean-up can make the playing area free of potential hazards and at the same time get you in touch with the layout of the land and whatever holes, sprinkler heads, or other unexpected obstacles you'll want to work around in plotting areas for various games. When you know the general character of your site, you can begin to plan games and activities accordingly.

Games. Let the site work together with the games you'll be playing to create a unique play arena. While New Games can adapt themselves to almost any terrain (barring perhaps mountains or marshes), you should consider the size and shape of the area in relation to intended activities. For a worthy game of Tournament Earthball, for example, you will need a space at least fifty yards long. A creek running through the property will indicate where to arrange Tug of War. Three or four neighboring trees are the perfect place to string a rope for a Boffing ring. Take into account that activities may have to be rotated during the course of the tournament to prevent damage to any particular area.

All free-form games should take place in a broad central portion of the site. Although you may want to label certain parts of it for scheduled events, avoid placing unnecessary physical boundaries or barriers between games. Activities will define their own spaces, and the absence of boundaries will encourage players to flow freely from game to game.

You shouldn't try to plan a specific time and place for every game, but it is helpful to post a schedule of times and places for key game events. Games like Tug of War and Tournament Earthball, which require many people, are good to schedule, as well as events like the Lap Game if you are going to try for a record-breaking sitting. For those who may be shy to enter games freely, scheduled events provide an encouraging invitation. You may also want to list the other games that will be happening spontaneously

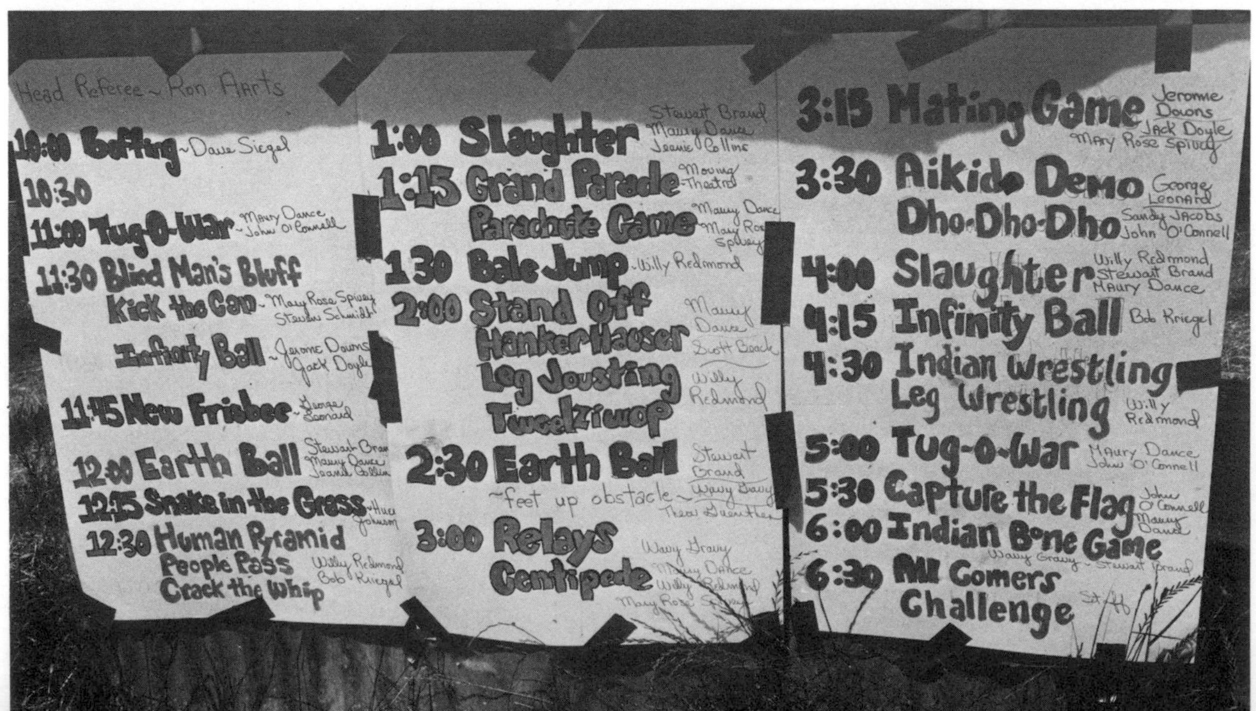

throughout the day as an overview and introduction to the event. This list also makes a handy touchstone for referees and players when memory and ingenuity have temporarily fled.

Once you have prepared and posted your schedule, be ready to dispense with it and flow with the interests and ideas of the participants. You will find that games you think will take five minutes will end up going strong for forty-five, and vice versa. The main purpose of the schedule is to ensure players a variety of simultaneous options.

Make sure there are gentle games like the Bone Game and Spirals, one-on-one games like Stand-Off and Boffing, and group events of varying activity levels. Whatever games you decide upon, it is essential that they suit your spectrum of players. Be sure to have games that the whole family can play together, as well as games that offer challenge to the neighborhood jock.

Activities. On the periphery of the site, surrounding the play area, locate all crafts activities, booths, displays, services, and other events that need defined spaces. In the arts and crafts sections, people can build kites and stilts, paint faces, make masks from gauze and paste, participate in group murals, weavings, and sculptures, and create musical instruments.

While minstrels, magicians, jugglers, mimes, and clowns will wander throughout the site, this area on the periphery can present other performing arts activities and demonstrations—puppet shows and a shadow theater, belly dancers, aikido and other martial arts, folk and free-form dancing, and music. We have found that acoustic (as opposed to amplified) music is best at a New Games tournament, for it contributes to the atmosphere but does not dominate it.

Besides these activities, the design of structures on the site can create an air of spectacle and pageantry that conveys the feeling of something special happening. You may want to raise a large banner as a focus for the tournament, fill the air with kites, balloons, and flags, and schedule parades.

A theme can serve as an inspiration for design of the site and

a focus for determining activities. If your theme is a historical holiday, you might resurrect some games popular in the period you are celebrating and tailor other games to fit. If your theme is cultural or ethnic, you could play Piedra/Papel/Tijeras instead of Rock/Paper/Scissors. For an environmental theme, emphasize endangered species in the Mating Game, create a game based on identifying plants or animals, or set up a display of wildlife native to your area, as we did for the Second Tournament.

Services. *Everyone at the tournament is creating a community for that time—a play community. Arranging for vital services is merely providing for that community's needs. You might encourage people to bring their own picnic lunches, but you may also want to provide a food service on the site. A simple, wholesome meal would be most in keeping with the grassroots attitude of New Games. Ethnic foods can express your chosen theme, give groups the opportunity to participate in the event, and perhaps contribute to the funding of the tournament as well. In considering food services, check your access to electrical power outlets and whether you have sufficient power to sustain the services. If not, portable generators fueled by gas are an alternative. Federal and local regulations on food preparation and the license to sell should be checked out beforehand, as well as additional liability coverage on your insurance.*

Providing cold drinking water for people who are playing hard is one of the best services you can perform. If fountains or facilities on the site are not sufficient, often the Army or National Guard can supply water in large field tanks. Construction companies might share their facilities or companies who bottle spring or distilled water might contribute.

Depending on the site, you will need to either provide access to restrooms or furnish portable toilets. Approximately one toilet for every 500 persons is sufficient, but it's preferable to overestimate. Our greatest fear in preparing for the Third Tournament in San Francisco was that thousands of people would turn out for the event and we wouldn't have enough sanitary facilities.

Careful preparation for all emergencies will pay off with peace of mind. For a small event, this is relatively simple, but for a large event, preparations for emergency services must be more complete. Before the event, alert local public services—the fire department, the nearest hospital, the sheriff's office, and the highway patrol—to allow them to be in a state of readiness to respond to any emergencies you may have. Know where the nearest telephone is located and secure permission to use it. In lieu of this, provide for walkie-talkies or other communication devices. Know the location of the nearest hospital and decide who will provide transportation, if necessary. For large groups—1000 or more—an ambulance should be on the site.

Be prepared to deal with minor emergencies by having on hand a fire extinguisher, security personnel, and at least one person at the event trained in first-aid. The Red Cross and other public agencies can provide someone suitable, but in many areas they require substantial advance notice. (In San Francisco, this is thirty days.) Establish a first-aid center on the periphery of the site, clearly marked with a sign or poster. All tournament officials, including referees, organizers, and police, should be clear on emergency procedures and the location of the first-aid shelter.

You should place your information booth in a location that is central and easily accessible. This vital service is the hub of your event, and you might want to distinguish it with a banner or other attractive identification. Those staffing the booth should know the location of all services at the event, the schedule of games, and be able to answer the questions of people interested in New Games and how the tournament was organized. Have a sign-up list available there for those who are interested in more information and further contact.

One aspect of New Games is that participants take on responsibility for themselves and their environment. Certainly you should notify police about the event and inform them of the logistics—the time, the site, and what will be happening. But in effect, the referees and players themselves police the event. Referees fulfill this function by directing the energy center away from disruptions and dealing with problems quietly. Security personnel on the site should be encouraged to be as much a part of the tournament as possible.

Environment. Invite participants to join in caring for the environment. A statement posted at the entrance to the site can help remind people to respect the grass and trees and to be aware of their own part in keeping the area beautiful. Since a list of do's and don't's generally elicits the inverse response, be creative and choose perhaps an American Indian poem about the earth or a humorous message with a familiar hero, like Snoopy, gathering up the trash.

Have brightly decorated trash cans located throughout the

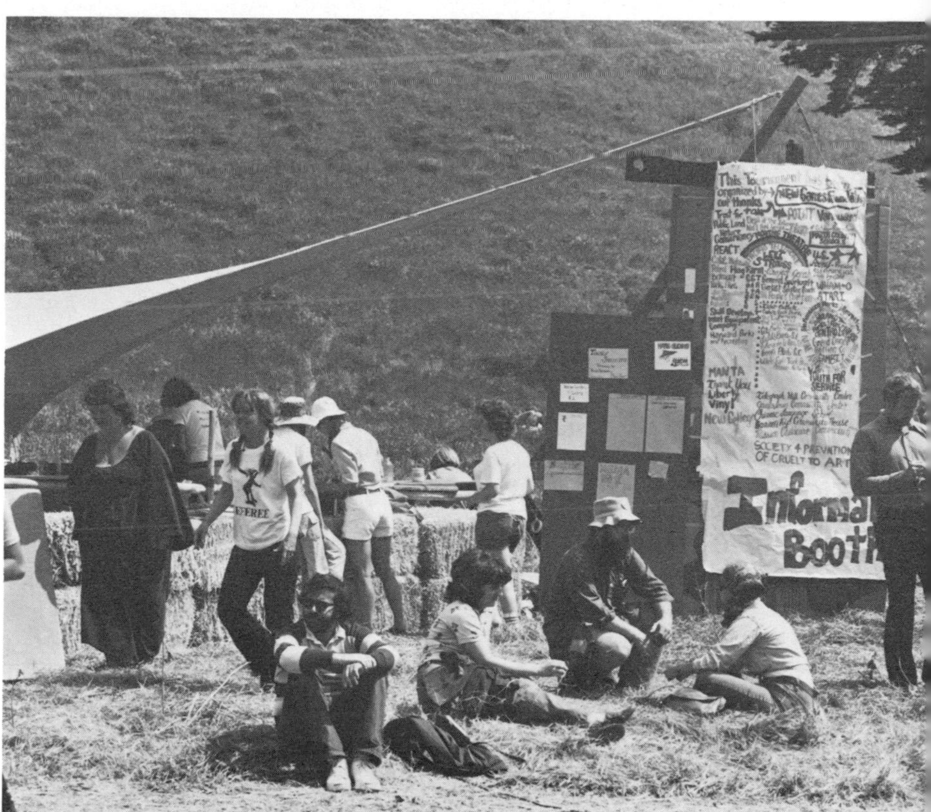

area and make clear arrangements for waste disposal. If you gauge before the tournament what kinds of trash there most likely will be (food and beverage containers, for example) you will know whether or not it will be necessary to empty the barrels during the event. Be sure to have a vehicle to transport the refuse you collect, and contact your local dump to find out its location, hours, and how much they charge for receiving each load. Cans and bottles can be brought to your local recycling center.

Although referees and players can complete a scouring of the site at the end of the tournament, clean-up should be continuous so that everyone gets the chance to contribute. Have plenty of plastic bags and trash barrels available. With imagination, the process can be creative and playful—supply paints for decorating the barrels, invent a game of litter tag, exchange donated equipment for bulging bags of garbage. You might even encourage collectors to draw upon their other talents to build a garbage sculpture that grows throughout the day until evening, when it first becomes the Eco-Ball goal post and later the target for a demolition derby.

Materials. *Limitations on material resources can generate enthusiasm and ingenuity on the part of both organizers and contributors. You might find yourselves able to use what others have found useless. Businesses, for instance, might provide their second-quality materials to the event. If you cannot borrow equipment, try to purchase it at a reduced cost. Remember, New Games equipment is not necessarily sports equipment. Accept what anyone offers and trust the imagination of the players to create a new game with it. (For more information on equipment, see page 190.)*

Contact people in person for contributions. Show them this book or the New Games film. Leave with them written information about New Games and about your own proposed tournament. You will sell the idea of the tournament to those you are approaching as you embody the essence of the New Games concept yourself and make them a part of it as well. Enjoy what you are doing—play with people you are approaching. One of our staff brought along Boffers to his meeting with the local newspaper. Boffing in the aisles of their office convinced them that this was an event they wanted to publicize.

Let contributors know how the tournament can benefit them as well as the community at large. By posting on the site the names of all contributing organizations and individuals, you will be increasing their visibility in the community. Label loaned or donated items with the names of the contributors. Introduce them to the media before and during the event. Let the community know who is helping to create the tournament. Invite them all to a pre-event publicity gathering at which they can meet each other. Be sure to keep a list of all contacts and contributors and distribute it to those who are interested. This network can serve the community in many ways long after the tournament is over.

Funding. *Those who cannot contribute their time or material resources migh be interested in providing funding for* *the event. Contact businesses, corporations, and foundations. City recreation departments and other governmental agencies may find the event a legitimate extension of their own programs and also provide funding. Some of the expenditures your budget may have to cover are:*

Office supplies
Publicity and printing
Postage
Photography
Insurance (a major item)
Consultation (if you work with the New Games Foundation)
Rental fees on structures and equipment
Vehicles and machinery to transport equipment and set up the site
Materials to contribute to on-site ambiance
Crafts and games supplies
Waste disposal
Salaries

Most of these expenditures will be affected by the extent to which you receive volunteer help and donations.

The sale of food or crafts at the tournament can help defray expenses as well. As a last resort, the players themselves can participate in the funding by paying an admission price or giving a donation. However, as we have discovered, free admission better suits the nature of a New Games event, so that players can be drawn in spontaneously as the games intrigue them and leave as they wish, and families do not find themselves unable to participate because of the cost. If you do charge for arts and crafts activities, prices should always be more of an invitation than a demand.

Insurance. *There is no fixed standard for liability insurance for a tournament. It varies from one event to another and from city to city, depending on whether the site is private or public, what kinds of activities are scheduled, who is sponsoring the event, and the number of people involved. Since New Games events are still unusual phenomena, you might encounter some difficulty arranging for adequate insurance coverage at a reasonable cost. We would hope that as more communities stage their own events and insurance companies understand how different New Games is from traditional sports activities, comprehensive insurance will be easier to arrange. Get in touch with a local insurance broker, interest him or her in New Games, and work creatively together to shape a policy that suits your needs.*

Publicity. *The number of people you wish to draw to an event can be controlled by the extent of your publicity and the types of media you choose to use. For example, some people might never look at newspapers but they watch television or read posters at the grocery store. For maximum contact, utilize television, radio, and newspapers as well as posting announcements and mailing out flyers. In developing your publicity campaign, remember that New Games events grow from the bottom up. Rather than placing a display ad in the newspapers, for example, talk to someone about running feature stories before the event.*

Prepare a press packet containing information on New Games and the tournament, including photographs, posters and flyers, and any official endorsements you may have received. (For instance, in the

Bay Area, several mayors have proclaimed an official New Games Day.) Approach both college and city newspapers and public and private radio stations. Present the tournament on talk shows and news programs. Offer television stations the use of the New Games film or slides to illustrate your presentation. Announce the event in the community activities listings on educational television and the public service announcements on radio and in newspapers.

In your advertising, remember that you are contacting a broad spectrum of people—of varying ages, incomes, interests, and values. Let the people you are inviting know what to expect and what might be expected of them. It's especially important that everyone knows to wear an old pair of blue jeans to the event—they'll be much more likely to join in the fun if they're not afraid of getting grass stains on their trousers or letting their slips show.

Referees. *During the tournament, referees will fulfill the most vital functions. Besides facilitating games, they serve as supervisors, security personnel, information sources, and the link between the players and the organizers of the event.*

You can recruit referees from many different organizations in your community. In this way, players can become familiar with the people behind their community services, and those functioning as referees can bring New Games back into the community through their organizations. Be sure to draw upon a cross-section of people to serve as referees—high school and college athletes of both sexes, senior citizens, and people of varying physical abilities. Just as everyone can play New Games, everyone can referee them. You might even publicly announce the referee training session for everyone interested.

The number of referees you will need for an event depends, of course, on the size and nature of the group you expect. For a group that is predominantly children, you need about one referee for every ten, while for a group of interested adults, one referee per 200 could be sufficient. The more cooperative the group playing, the fewer referees will be needed. During the tournament, players will also take on the role of refereeing.

The referee training session before the tournament is a crucial experience for instilling referees with the spirit of New Games and with a comprehension of what they are about. A good set of referees who respect the concept and work well together will contribute immeasurably to the tone of the event. It is essential for all referees to have played New Games before the event. Once they have learned to let go when they play, yet take responsibility for the energy release they experience, they can encourage others to do so with understanding.

Supply referees with a reference sheet that they can put into their pockets. This can include safety factors, cleanup arrangements, reminders to change rules, a list of games along with the times and locations of scheduled events, parts of the environment to be protected, emergency procedures, and a map of the area. Referees, as all officials at a New

Games tournament, should be easily identifiable. T-shirts bearing the injunction to "Play Hard, Play Fair, Nobody Hurt" can be a good way to deal with this. (For further information on the role of the referee, see the article on page 83.)

The Event. *The last few days of preparation before the tournament will be unavoidably hectic. Just trust that if you have given your best, everything essential to the event will be accomplished. During the tournament, remember that everyone there is helping to create it, and you are free to join in the fun. If everything is not turning out exactly as you had imagined, it will undoubtedly be turning out better.*

In the afterglow of the tournament, you can sit back and consider that what happened was not just an event in time. People are now acquainted with a new tool to work with in their own groups. And even more than that, they have been introduced to the larger community of which they are a part. The tournament has not only served as a forum for people to play together—it has served as a focus for community action.

The real measure of your tournament's success is not likely to become evident until long after the event itself. It might happen at a City Council meeting at which two speakers are presenting opposing views. When one recognizes the other and exclaims, "Oh, I stood next to you in the People Pass," you'll know that your tournament worked. And when the other responds, "Yes, we ought to have another New Games tournament," you'll know that it's still working. ■

188 **THE GAME OF GAMES** An athlete in the Game of Games is one who plays life intensely, with heightened awareness of this endeavor. An athlete is one who can perceive discord and harmony both, who can accept contradiction as the very stuff of play while not losing sight of the ultimate harmony. An athlete in this Game plays voluntarily and wholeheartedly, even while realizing that this Game is not all that is; knows the rules and limitations of play, and sees beauty in the order thus imposed; seeks to expand any frontier available and yet is not unmindful of ethical imperatives and the needs of others. This athlete contends in a game for a prize, and the prize is play itself, a life fully experienced and examined.

The athlete in the Game of Games may be a musician or a carpenter, a householder or a yogi, an Olympic runner or a farmer. No one can be excluded merely because of occupational specialty, and differences between the purely physical and nonphysical begin to fade. It is only through a heresy in Western thought that we could consider any aspect of life as "nonphysical." The body is always involved, even in what we call the most cerebral pursuit. Einstein tells us that the Special or Restricted Theory of Relativity came from a feeling in his muscles. Surely he was a great athlete of the Game of Games, in which we are all embodied. Embodiment is indeed the primary condition of play. When Western philosophy and theology attempted to cut away the body from the Higher Life, the Life of the Mind, the attempt failed. The body, unacknowledged, remained a part of every formulation. To the precise extent that it has been ignored, Western thought has become fragmentary and misleading.

Spirit in flesh, flesh in spirit. Abstractions in the muscles, visions in the bones. We can no longer deny the conditions of embodiment—nor can we ever entirely explain them. However far we pursue the mystery, it finally eludes us. The "answer" lies in the unsayable statement, the unprovable proposition that prevents paradox and foreclosure. There are no closed systems. The body opens us to wonders in this and other worlds. Its movements through space and time can launch us on a timeless voyage to a place beyond place. **GEORGE LEONARD**

George Leonard, author, lecturer, and New Games enthusiast, has written several books including *Education and Ecstacy*, *The Transformation*, and *The Ultimate Athlete* ($8.95, Viking Press), from which this essay is excerpted. He holds a black belt in aikido.

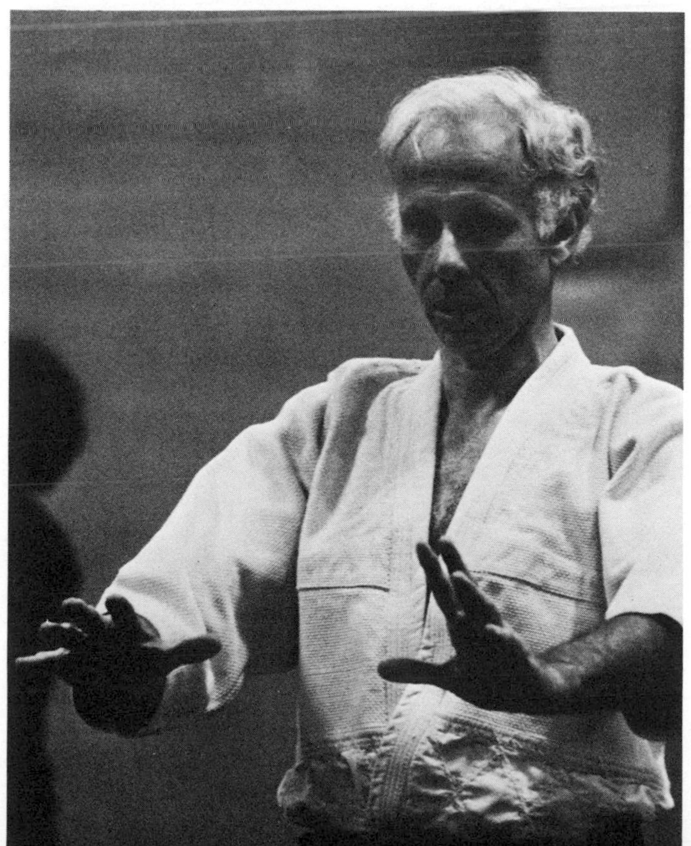

NEW GAMES EQUIPMENT YOU DON'T REALLY NEED

Most of the games in this book can be played without any special equipment. All you need is some open space and willing people. The amount of fun you have isn't dependent on how much equipment you've got.

What follows is a listing of the few items which you might not be able to find around your home or neighborhood, or for minimal cost at your local variety store. For the items below which are commercially produced, we'll be keeping abreast of the best sources—highest quality for least cost. If you'd like the latest information on how to obtain these, write to the New Games Foundation, P.O. Box 7901, San Francisco, California 94120. (Please enclose a self-addressed, stamped envelope so we can reply speedily.)

Earthballs. Sold by recreation equipment manufacturers as cage balls or push balls, the basic ball has a canvas cover and a vinyl bladder and is six feet in diameter. It becomes an Earthball when the whole earth is painted on the outside (use alcohol-base paints or Inko dyes). Earthballs are sturdy toys and will last for years. They cost about $200. If your organization or community would like to purchase one, check with the New Games Foundation for the best sources.

Parachutes. The number of games a group can play with a parachute is limited only by the imagination. A useful chute can range in size from 24 to 32 feet in diameter and might cost from $50 to $200 for a used one. Look around in army surplus stores or check with local airports and military bases. Avoid cargo chutes (too heavy) and look for ones with multi-colored panels.

Fraha / Las Paletas. Several comp[illegible]s make the equipment for this paddle-and-ball game. They sell sets with two paddles and a couple of balls for about $10. You can make your own set by cutting two paddle shapes (nine inches in diameter with five-inch long handles) out of half-inch plywood. Glue two pieces of half-round moulding to the handles. The commercial sets are supplied with squash balls, but you can create your own version by experimenting with different balls.

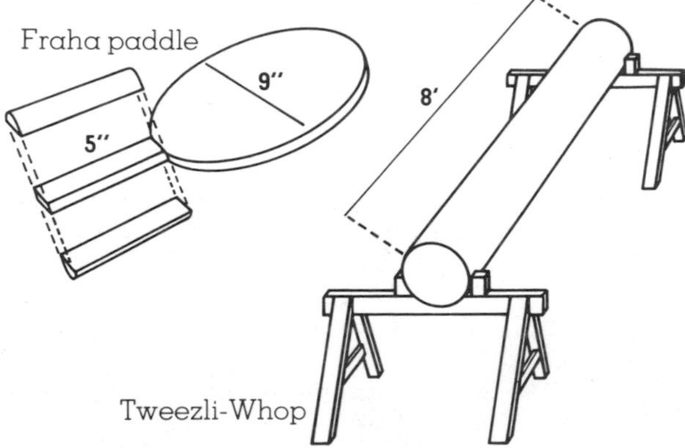

Tweezli-Whop. To play this game (see page 23 for game rules), you'll need a round balance beam with a pile of hay beneath it. A simple, portable Tweezli-Whop set-up can be made with two sawhorses of equal size, a telephone pole about eight feet long covered with a sheet of plastic (to make it slippery and splinterless), and four blocks of wood nailed on the horses to hold the beam in place. Get several bales of hay from a stable, stuff some of it into two burlap sacks or laundry bags, and distribute the rest generously under and around the beam. Whop away!

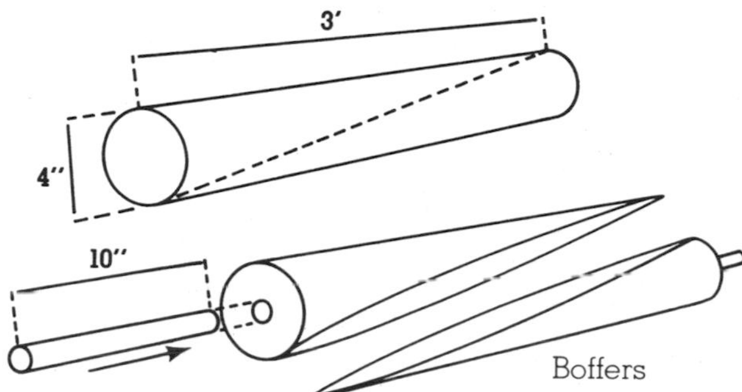

Boffers

Boffers. Commercially produced Boffers are made of triangular-shaped polyethylene foam wedges with plastic handles and come supplied with plastic goggles and doughnut shaped, polyethylene ear protectors. They cost about $14 for a pair. You can make your own set of "no fault" duelling sabres by getting a four-inch by three-foot cylinder of polyethylene foam from a packaging supply company (check your Yellow Pages under "Plastics—Foam"). Slice the cylinder diagonally with a hacksaw or serrated knife to make two tapered, semi-circular forms. Punch holes in the ends of the forms, and insert one-inch diameter wooden dowels, cut to ten inches in length, about five inches into each of the forms. (The best way to get the dowels to adhere to the polyethylene is to heat them almost until burning and plunge them into the forms so the foam melts.) Cover the dowels with bicycle grips or wrap with tape. Before you start Boffing, don't forget to get some eye protectors from a sports supply store.

Tug of War Ropes. A one-inch thick rope is the minimum thickness for a good Tug of War rope (thin ropes cause rope burns and break easily). If you want a rope more than fifty feet long (and you plan on having more than fifty feet of people pulling on it), get one that's two inches thick. You'll need a three-inch rope for a tug over two hundred feet long. Three-inch manila rope sometimes can be obtained from shipping companies or naval surplus stores, although it's likely to be expensive. Two-inch synthetic rope is very strong and lightweight, and is available from cordage companies, athletic supply houses, and marine supply stores.

Referee T-Shirts. The perfect way to get everyone into the Player-Referee spirit is with a New Games referee T-shirt. They're available from the New Games Foundation, or you can make your own, but don't forget to put "Play Hard, Play Fair, Nobody Hurt" on the back. ■

NEW GAMES... AND MORE!

Page numbers in *italic* type refer to *The New Games Book*.
Page numbers in roman type refer to *More New Games!*

	High Activity	*Medium Activity*	*Low Activity*
Games for Two	Boffing *25*	Butt Off 23	Aura *37*
	Crab Grab 15	Fraha *33*	Commons 25
	Human Spring 17	Hunker Hawser *31*	Frisbee Golf *39*
	Schmerltz *27*	Me Switch 19	Last Detail 29
	Toe Fencing 13	New Frisbee *29*	Stand-Off *35*
	Tweezli-Whop *23*	Quick Draw 21	This Is My Nose 27
Games for a Dozen	Bola *49*	Ball Crawl *67*	A What? 73
	Catch the Dragon's Tail *47*	Behavior Modification 63	The Bone Game *79*
	Flying Dutchman *45*	Fox and Squirrel *59*	Egg Toss *75*
	Frisbee Fakeout 47	Group Juggling 61	Instant Replay 71
	Go-Tag *53*	How Do You Do? 57	Killer 81
	Human Pinball *51*	People Pyramids *57*	Knots *69*
	Samurai Warrior 51	Pieing *63*	Lummi Sticks *73*
	Star Wars 55	Pile Up 65	Mime Rhyme 83
	Swat 45	Pushpin Soccer 69	Name Train 75
	Taffy Pull 49	Smaug's Jewels *61*	Rattlers *77*
	Triangle Tag 43	Snowblind 59	Red Handed *71*
	Ultimate Nerf 53	Stand Up *65*	Sightless Sculpture 77
	Water Slide *55*	Willow in the Wind 67	Zen Clap 79
Games for Two Dozen	Blob *107*	Body Snatchers 125	Data Processing 139
	British Bulldog *105*	Body Surfing 133	Elephant/Palm Tree/Monkey 147
	Broken Spoke 105	Bug Tug *121*	Hagoo *135*
	Clam Free 113	Caterpillar *117*	Human Compressor 141
	Dho-Dho-Dho *97*	Cookie Machine 135	Islands *127*
	Elbow Tag 121	Hug Tag *115*	Knight's Move 137
	Great Plains *99*	Jamaquack 129	The Mating Game *125*
	Knock Your Socks Off 117	Lemonade 127	Ooh-Ahh *129*
	Loose Caboose 107	New Volleyball *113*	Pina *131*
	Monarch 115	Orbit *111*	Prui *133*
	Siamese Soccer *95*	Quick Lineup 131	Rain 149
	Snake-in-the-Grass *93*	Rock/Paper/Scissors *109*	Shoe Factory 143
	Slaughter/Annihilation *101*	Skin the Snake *119*	Tableaux 145
	Wink 109	Yurt Circle 123	Vampire *123*
The More the Better	Clench a Wench/Mensch *151*	Amoeba Race *159*	Eco-Ball *175*
	Earth Volley *155*	Chute Ball *165*	Get Down 179
	Earthball Games *143*, 162	Giants/Elves/Wizards 167	The Lap Game *171*
	Everybody's It 159	Parachute Games *161*, 173	Planet Pass *167*
	Octopus 157	People Pass *157*	Psychic Shake 177
	Space Chase 161	People to People 165	Spirals *169*
	Tug of War *153*	Swamp Chute 171	Vortex 175

It's Finally Here!

More New Games! is the book you've been waiting for. This companion volume to *The New Games Book* will take you even further into the joys of playing New Games with your friends, families, clients, and co-workers.

More New Games! offers a wealth of new material:

• Sixty of the best new New Games we've learned in the past five years, including such favorites as Me Switch, Clam Free, Octopus, and Get Down.

• Over two-hundred photographs of players across the country reinforcing our invitation to play.

• Essays describing what makes a game a New Game, suggestions for refereeing your games, capsule descriptions of several applications of New Games, and an update of what we're up to at the New Games Foundation.

More New Games! exemplifies the phenomenal growth of the New Games movement in the past five years. Through hundreds of trainings, workshops, and festivals, we've refined our approach to play and have learned, again and again, just how magical play can be.

More New Games! is written and photographed by Andrew Fluegelman in cooperation with the New Games Foundation, produced by The Headlands Press, and published by Doubleday & Co.

The New Games Foundation is a non-profit organization dedicated to the implementation of the concept of New Games. Through our office in San Francisco, California, we conduct workshops and play sessions and provide consulting services to individuals and organizations. We also maintain a mail-order sales program of our books and other play items.

The Foundation conducts two- and three-day training sessions across the country every spring. Professionals from such diverse fields as recreation, education, mental health, youth work, industrial recreation, and senior citizen programs have expanded their tools for working with people through a New Games Training. Participants work and play with the concept of New Games—exploring refereeing, game change and invention, and program application of New Games.

We also conduct group trainings on a contract basis for entire organizations. We can modify our basic training outline to meet special needs of the sponsoring organization. Group trainings are scheduled throughout the year.

The Foundation's mail-order sales program currently offers *The New Games Book*, *More New Games!*, Earthballs, playchutes, and a selection of T-shirts. Our slide show, "Play Hard, Play Fair, Nobody Hurt," is also available for rent. The *New Games Resource Catalog* is an annotated compilation of play ideas, books, equipment, and other resources.

"Friends of New Games" is the Foundation's membership program. Members share a belief in the value of play and support the Foundation through tax-deductible membership donations. Financial assistance is welcome and needed to explore new program directions for reaching more people.

For further information, please write the New Games Foundation, P.O. Box 7901, San Francisco, California 94120.

Special thanks to

Ron Aarts
Dave Aikman
Peter Armour
Fred Auda
Judy Auda
Susan Benson
Scott Bulkley
Adrienne Burk
Bill Burke
Robert Burkhardt
Pam Cleland
Cathy Crammer
Maury Dance
John Daniell
Bernie De Koven
Larry Diamond
John Dolinsek
Julia Robb Dorn
Peter Ellis
Brandie Farrington
Pat Farrington
Conger Fawcett
Meg Fawcett
Sandy Finnegan
Andrew Fluegelman
Laura Glicken
Andy Grimstad
Walt Handschin
Marc Hoffman
Susan Johnson
Joe Killian
Marty Krugman
Ken Leary
Dale LeFevre
Howard Levitt
Steve Meyer
Kathy Meyers
Trina Merriman
Bill Michaelis
Ray Murray
Carolyn Myers
Barbara Naiditch
Burton Naiditch
John O'Connell
Ivan Olsen
Louie Patler
Ronnie Paul
Julie Patterson
Gil Rusk
Sharon Skolnick
Nancy Smedley
Jan Spector
Todd Strong
Susan Sunderland
Michael Toms
Marcelle Weed
David Wiggins
Debrah Woodbey

What's Your New Game?

Do you have a favorite game you'd like to share?
Please let us know about it.
Or tell us about a variation of one of the games in this book.
We'll pass it along to the New Games community.

Name of game: ______________________________

How it's played:

☐ My organization is interested in sponsoring a group training.

☐ Enclosed is $1.00 for the *New Games Resource Catalog* that gives ordering information for:

- ☐ *More New Games!*
- ☐ Earthballs
- ☐ Playchutes
- ☐ T-shirts
- ☐ Slide-show rental
- ☐ Other books and play equipment

Name ______________________________

Address ______________________________

City ______________________________

State ______________ Zip ______________

Phone ______________________________

Organization ______________________________

My primary field of interest is:

☐ Recreation ☐ Business
☐ Education ☐ Health
☐ Youth ☐ Church
☐ Other ______________________________

Mail this form to:
New Games Foundation
P.O. Box 7901
San Francisco, California 94120

cut

fold

place
stamp
here

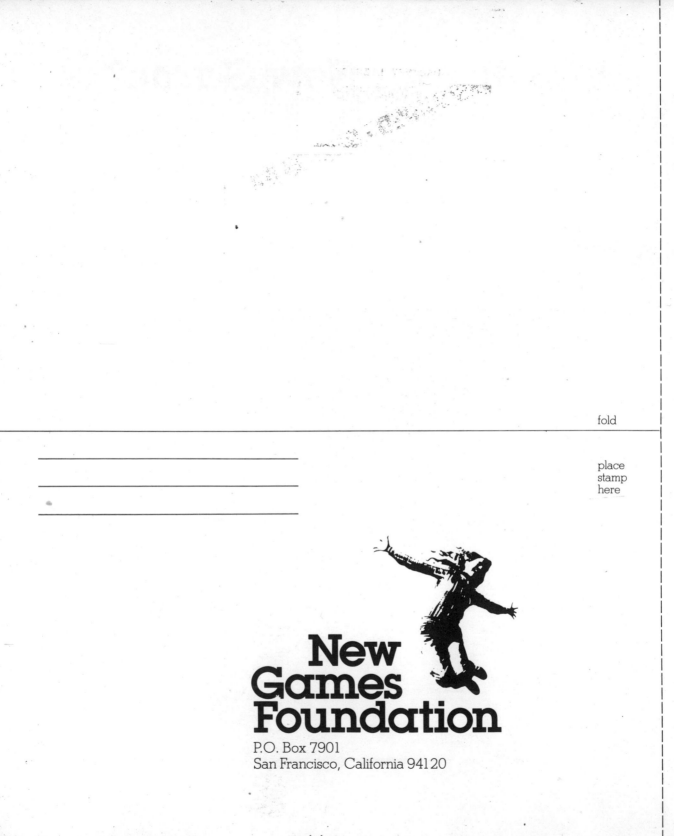

P.O. Box 7901
San Francisco, California 94120

staple here